DAM BUSTERS

FAILED TO RETURN

Published in 2013 by Fighting High Ltd, 23 Hitchin Road,
Stotfold, Hitchin, Herts, SG5 4HP
www.fightinghigh.com

British Library Cataloguing-in-Publication data. A CIP record
for this title is available from the British Library.

ISBN 978 0 9571163 4 4

Designed by Michael Lindley www.truthstudio.co.uk.
Printed and bound in China by Toppan Leefung.

DAM BUSTERS

FAILED TO RETURN

ROBERT OWEN, STEVE DARLOW, SEAN FEAST AND ARTHUR THORNING

FH

'IT IS IMPOSSIBLE TO FIND WORDS ADEQUATELY TO EXPRESS WHAT ONE FEELS ABOUT THE AIR CREWS. THE GALLANTRY WITH WHICH THEY GO INTO ACTION IS INCOMPARABLE. WHILE THE OLDER GENERATION OF AIR FORCE OFFICERS MAY NOT BE CALLED UPON TO CARRY OUT ACTUAL ATTACKS IN PERSON, THE SPIRIT OF THEIR JUNIORS MUST PROCEED FROM THEIR THOUGHT AND TRAINING, AND IN PRAISING YOUR CREWS I WOULD LIKE TO ADD THE THANKS WHICH I FEEL ARE DUE TO YOU AS ONE OF THE SENIOR OFFICERS OF THE AIR FORCE, FOR THE OUTSTANDING GENERATION OF PILOTS WHICH YOUR EXAMPLE AND TRAINING HAS PRODUCED. WILL YOU PLEASE ACCEPT THE DEEPEST SYMPATHY OF ALL OF US ON THE LOSSES WHICH THE SQUADRON HAS SUSTAINED. YOU WILL UNDERSTAND, I THINK, THE

133

NUMBER OF AIRCREW WHO TOOK PART
IN THE DAM BUSTERS RAID

19

NUMBER OF AIRCRAFT THAT TOOK PART
IN THE DAM BUSTERS RAID

TREMENDOUS STRAIN WHICH I FELT AT HAVING BEEN THE CAUSE OF SENDING THESE CREWS ON SO PERILOUS A MISSION, AND THE TENSE MOMENTS IN THE OPERATIONS ROOM, WHEN, AFTER FOUR ATTACKS, I FELT THAT I HAD FAILED TO MAKE GOOD, WERE ALMOST MORE THAN I COULD BEAR; AND FOR ME THE SUBSEQUENT SUCCESS WAS ALMOST COMPLETELY BLOTTED OUT BY THE SENSE OF LOSS OF THOSE WONDERFUL YOUNG LIVES. IN THE LIGHT OF OUR SUBSEQUENT KNOWLEDGE I DO HOPE THAT ALL THOSE CONCERNED WILL FEEL THAT THE RESULTS ACHIEVED HAVE NOT RENDERED THEIR SACRIFICE IN VAIN.'

(BARNES WALLIS TO AVM SIR RALPH COCHRANE)

8
NUMBER OF AIRCRAFT THAT FAILED TO RETURN FROM THE RAID

53
NUMBER OF AIRMEN KILLED ON THE RAID

CONTENTS

65

46

62

119

30

85

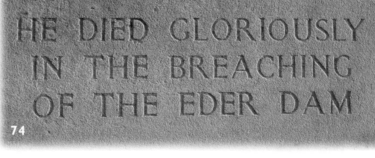

HE DIED GLORIOUSLY
IN THE BREACHING
OF THE EDER DAM
74

20

113

76

101

INTRODUCTION

BY ROBERT OWEN

ON THE NIGHT of 16/17 May 1943 nineteen Lancasters of No. 617 Squadron were despatched from RAF Scampton to execute an audacious low-level raid against the major dams of western Germany. The Dams Raid, or, to give it its official title, Operation Chastise, is regarded as one of the greatest feats of arms ever performed by the Royal Air Force.

Operation Chastise

By the spring of 1943, under the leadership of Air Chief Marshal Sir Arthur Harris, Bomber Command was a potent weapon poised to take the Allies' war into the industrial heart of Germany. While increasingly effective bombing operations would disrupt the production of war materiel, a daring plan was coming to fruition that had been many years in preparation – to breach major dams in Western Germany, whose reservoirs provided much of the water supply for its armament manufacturers and industrial workforce.

To achieve this objective, a unique weapon had been developed by Barnes Wallis, Vickers Armstrong's assistant chief designer. Code-named 'Upkeep', this was a large cylindrical mine that, when released from low level with backspin imparted prior to release, would strike the water of the reservoir, and then ricochet across the surface towards the dam in a series of decreasing bounces, thereby defeating any conventional net defences. On striking the wall it would sink, the backspin causing it to remain in contact with the masonry, until it reached 30 feet in depth, where three hydrostatic pistols would detonate a charge of 6,600 lb of RDX.

The dams had to be attacked when the reservoirs were at their fullest, with the greatest pressure acting on the dams, and coincident with a full moon to facilitate a night attack. This established a date no later than 26 May. When Wallis was given the green light to develop a full-scale weapon on 26 February, Upkeep had performed only as a scaled-down prototype – dropped by a Wellington in the waters off Chesil Beach. Although these smaller models had demonstrated that theory would translate into practice, there was still much development to ensure that the full-scale weapon would perform in the desired manner. While Wallis was driven by his own tenacity, self-belief and faith in his calculations, neither he nor anyone else had the benefit of hindsight to know that the larger weapon would work.

Left Barnes Wallis
(*IWM HU 92132*)

One of the targets:
the Möhne Dam
before the Second
World War (from an
easterly direction).
(*Air Historical Branch*)

Right The Eder Dam
pictured prior to the
raid of 16/17 May
1943. (*Air Historical
Branch*)

For this reason, combined with an inherent mistrust of inventors and their promises, and eschewing what he considered 'panacea targets', Harris had railed against Wallis's proposal, writing that this was 'the maddest proposition of a weapon that we have come across' and that its protagonists should be 'given one aeroplane and told to go away and play while we get on with the war'. He was overruled by Air Chief Marshal Sir Charles Portal, Chief of the Air Staff, and was only slightly mollified by Portal's statement that 'only three of your precious Lancasters' – the only aircraft capable of modification to carry Upkeep – would be diverted until the idea was proven. In the event a total of twenty-three aircraft would be modified.

Realizing that he had no option, and with less than two months in which to train crews, Harris applied himself to the task with his customary zeal. Although the final release parameters had yet to be determined, delivery of the weapon would require a high degree of airmanship, necessitating an intense period of training to develop and perfect the specialist technique required. Harris was reluctant to take an established squadron out of the front-line units, which were about to engage in what would become the Battle of the Ruhr. In any case it was unlikely that any single squadron would be comprised entirely of crews with the required potential or experience.

Perhaps he also saw this as an opportunity to begin the expansion of his force, as it was decreed that a new squadron should be formed as part of Bomber Command's all Lancaster No. 5 Group, which was based in Lincolnshire and commanded by Air Vice Marshal Sir Ralph Cochrane. Cochrane had served under Harris in Mesopotamia during the 1920s, developing bombing accuracy with Vickers Vernons. As a former RNAS airship pilot, he had

Left An aerial reconnaissance photograph of the Möhne Dam before the 16/17 May 1943 raid, taken earlier in the year. (*Air Historical Branch*)

previously worked alongside Wallis at the Vickers works at Barrow-in-Furness and Howden.

The order to form the new squadron was issued on 17 March 1943. It was to be commanded by Wing Commander Guy Gibson, DSO, DFC, an experienced bomber and nightfighter pilot and protégé of Harris. Gibson had previously commanded No. 106 Squadron at RAF Syerston, by degrees transforming it into something of a specialist squadron, which had been given various new equipment to trial, including the Stabilized Automatic Bomb Sight and Capital Ship Bomb.

Contrary to legend, the crews were not all tour-expired, bemedalled veterans handpicked by Gibson, although without doubt his influence contributed to the selection of a number of former 106 aircrew – notably Flight Lieutenants John Hopgood and David Shannon and Pilot Officer Lewis Burpee. Others were known by repute, such

as Australian Flight Lieutenant 'Mick' Martin. No. 5 Group postings would doubtless have provided further advice, suggesting crews that had recently completed or were nearing the end of their tour, and some that were commencing their second tour. Nevertheless, it was important to maintain a balance and not to denude every squadron of its most experienced personnel, thereby weakening front-line strength. To leaven the mix, some crews were also selected who, despite not having vast operational experience, were assessed as being above average or who had demonstrated 'press-on' spirit. Harris's plans not to divert an entire squadron were partially undermined by the total transfer of the recently formed 'C' Flight of No. 57 Squadron to the new unit, despite protests by two captains, Pilot Officer Geoff Rice and Flight Sergeant Ray Lovell. In several cases, including Squadron Leader Melvin Young, Flight Lieutenant Hopgood and

Gibson himself, crews were assembled from disparate aircrew members, many of whom had not previously flown together. There were some unusual choices: Squadron Leader Young, the senior flight commander, and Flight Lieutenant Bill Astell had little experience of the Lancaster or the air war over Germany, having served mainly with Wellington units in the Middle East.

Twenty-one crews began to arrive at the designated base at Scampton, 5 miles north of Lincoln, on 25 March. Still a grass airfield, Scampton was about to be closed for the laying of concrete runways and was home to only one squadron, No. 57, which allowed the new squadron to form and train in relative obscurity. Many of the official channels struggled to keep up, so rapid was the squadron's formation – equipment had to be scrounged from the station and No. 57 Squadron. To begin with the squadron had no number. In *Enemy Coast Ahead*, Wing Commander Gibson referred to his new unit as Squadron 'X'. Although this is the traditional symbol for an unknown quantity, or element of mystery, in reality the letter carried no such overtones, being in keeping with standard nomenclature for newly forming units (X, Y and Z if more than one) until a number was allotted. Within a few days Scampton's new unit had become No. 617 Squadron, following on from the 600–16 Series allocated to Auxiliary Air Force Units. Its sister unit, No. 618 Squadron, was a Mosquito squadron formed in Coastal Command for a projected attack against *Tirpitz* using Highball, the anti-shipping version of Upkeep; paving the way for further expansion No. 619 Squadron would be formed as a standard Lancaster unit in No. 5 Group on 18 April.

Gibson's key task was to initiate training as quickly as possible, although he had no knowledge of either the intended target or the dropping technique required. He had been briefed only that the squadron would need to be able to navigate accurately at low level over enemy territory in moonlight to approach the target at 100 feet and at about 240 mph. 'It will be convenient to practise this over water.' Training commenced on 27 March, using standard Lancasters supplied by other units. Accurate navigation and low-level flying were addressed in the first stage, aircraft being sent on daylight cross-countries, in pairs at first, then singly,

following a number of established routes, which both served to make life easy for the Observer Corps and would take the crews to appropriate waypoints. Flying at 500 feet, techniques were developed that evolved as the height was progressively reduced to 100 feet. Low flying was demanding on both aircrew and aircraft. Recording his first low-level flight on 1 April, Sergeant Tom Maynard, gunner with Pilot Officer Geoff Rice, noted that it was very bumpy in the heavy wind. Two days later this crew would lose its trailing aerial, torn off as it snagged an obstacle at low level, the first of a number of mishaps to be experienced by the squadron during training. By the time operational aircraft modified to carry Upkeep were ready, these initial Lancasters would be showing their age, with popped rivets and wrinkled skin from the turbulence at low level. Minor incidents were not infrequent, with aircraft losing trailing aerials and returning with dented panels and foliage in intakes or around the tail wheel. Flight Lieutenant Norman Barlow collided with a bird, which shattered his windscreen, causing him to clip a tree.

Night cross-countries commenced on 10 April for a period of the full moon, but, in order to increase the amount of practice, four aircraft were fitted with a synthetic night-flying system known as 'two-stage amber'. Navigation was carried out largely by the bomb aimer using roller maps, with other crew members keeping watch for obstructions and landmarks.

By the beginning of April Wing Commander Gibson had been informed of his key targets, but the remainder of the squadron would continue to train without knowing the real nature of their objectives until they were revealed at briefing. (Their key targets were to be the Möhne and Sorpe Dams, providing water for the industrial area of the Ruhr, and the Eder Dam, which controlled the levels of the rivers Fulda and Weser, and the Mittelland Canal.)

Achieving the stringent release parameters required faultless teamwork. The pilot set up the line of attack, while the range was established using a triangulation principle, aligning two marks of the sight with the dam's two towers. Bomb aimers made their own variations of sight using either wood and nails, or a length of string and china-graph marks on the Perspex. To facilitate practice, in achieving the correct combination of height, speed and range necessary for release, targets representing the towers were erected on the dam at Eyebrook Reservoir, Uppingham, later moved to the Wainfleet bombing range on the Wash.

Height was determined using a device resurrected from the First World War: the spotlight altimeter calibrator. An Aldis lamp was fitted in the position normally occupied by the bombing camera, with a second one on the centre line, angled to intersect with the first at the required height beneath the aircraft. The navigator looked out of the cockpit blister and issued instructions to the pilot. Speed was the responsibility of the flight engineer, while the wireless operator operated a hydraulic valve to control the mine's speed of rotation, monitored by a rev counter mounted at the end of the navigator's table. By early May crews were determined to be proficient at navigation and bombing and were being sent on cross-countries involving runs over the reservoirs at Uppingham, Abberton and the Derwent Valley.

Meanwhile, while the squadron was perfecting its technique, Wallis was at Reculver, Kent, conducting concurrent trials, using Vickers and Avro test pilots, to determine precise release parameters for the full scale weapon. These began on 13 April but were initially unsuccessful, the weapon shattering on impact. It was less than three weeks before the operation that it was discovered, by progressive deduction, that, by dispensing with the wooden staves, a bare cylinder spun at 500 rpm, released from 60 feet at 235 mph, would consistently demonstrate the required performance.

The squadron began receiving its specially modified Lancasters to carry Upkeep from 8 April. With its mid-upper turret and bomb doors removed, the aircraft had the look of a gutted fish. Upkeep was carried clamped transversely between two spring-loaded V-shaped arms that sprang apart for release. To impart spin to the weapon, a hydraulic motor mounted in the forward part of the bomb bay was linked by a belt drive to a driving pulley on the starboard arm. Other modifications included the installation of VHF radio, enabling Wing Commander Gibson to control the operation by direct speech over the target – the forerunner of the Master Bomber technique.

With the design of the weapon and dropping technique finalized, the squadron undertook a series of drops at Reculver on 11–12 May, running in at right angles to the coast, east of the ruins of St Mary's Church. Unable to use the spotlight altimeter in daylight, several crews, including Flight Lieutenants Les Munro and 'Mick' Martin, released from below 60 feet. The resulting waterspout, thrown up by Upkeep's initial impact struck their aircraft, fortunately without causing major harm. Squadron Leader Henry Maudslay suffered likewise, the water tearing off panels and damaging the Lancaster's tail surfaces. On return to base the aircraft was found to be too severely damaged to take part in the operation.

By 13 May all was ready – and not a day too soon, since the last possible date for the raid had now been brought forward to 19 May. Last-minute changes were still being made. The attack profile on the Sorpe Dam was altered – aircraft would now run across the lake, at 180 mph as low as practicable, 30 feet out from the dam and release at its centre without spinning the mine. On the evening of 14 May most of the crews participated in what was loosely described as a dress rehearsal: those detailed for the main targets made runs at Eyebrook and Abberton reservoirs, those detailed for the Sorpe went to the Derwent Valley, and others carried out tactical and spotlight runs over the sea. On the 15th, flight commanders and section leaders were briefed by Gibson and Wallis, and the following day briefing of the crews began in earnest. Section leaders prepared their teams in the morning, with the crews seeing the targets early in the afternoon, with a final summary briefing for all, attended by Wallis and Cochrane, at which the former gave a short résumé of the weapon and its intended effect.

After the briefing was over crews adjourned for the customary pre-operation meal of bacon and eggs, prior to going down to flights to collect their flying clothing and rations. Only nineteen crews would be operating. Two were ostensibly out owing to sickness, although, with three aircraft being used for trials, and one having been seriously damaged, the squadron had only nineteen aircraft, until one

OPERATION CHASTISE - 16/17 MAY 1943
PRINCIPAL DAMS, ROUTES, AND LOSS LOCATIONS

RAF
Scampton

First Wave

Second and Third Waves

AJ-K

AJ-A

No. 617 Squadron Losses
AJ-K (P/O Byers)
AJ-A (S/Ldr Young)
AJ-S (P/O Burpee)
AJ-Z (S/Ldr Maudslay)
AJ-E (F/Lt Barlow)
AJ-B (F/Lt Astell)
AJ-C (P/O Ottley)
AJ-M (F/Lt Hopgood)

AJ-S   AJ-Z   AJ-B
Rees   AJ-E   AJ-C   AJ-M

Duisberg   Möhne Dam
Essen Dortmund

Sorpe Dam

Eder Dam

Main Image
Modern photograph of the Möhne Dam from the south-east.

Left A practice 'Upkeep' bomb attached to a modified Lancaster during the trial period prior to Chastise *(Air Historical Branch)*

To prevent confusion, for the purpose of this work, Waves are numbered in the order in which they took off.

Wave 1 (Sorpe Dam): Barlow, Munro, Byers, Rice, McCarthy.

Wave 2 (Möhne and Eder Dams): Gibson, Hopgood, Martin, Young, Shannon, Maltby, Maudslay, Astell, Knight.

Wave 3 (Reserve) Ottley, Burpee, Brown, Townsend, Anderson.

of the test aircraft was delivered to Scampton on the afternoon of 16 May, fortuitously providing a reserve.

The crews would depart in a number of waves. Five aircraft, each flying alone, would take a northern route, entering Holland across the Zuider Zee and heading for a point east of Rees, on the Rhine, where they would turn east to skirt north of the Ruhr before turning south for the Sorpe Dam. The second wave of nine aircraft, in three vics of three, each led by Wing Commander Gibson or a flight commander, would follow a southern route to the Scheldt Estuary, then up to Rees, where they would link with the northern route and head for the Möhne. Aircraft still with mines after successfully breaching this target would then proceed to attack the Eder.

The final wave of five would take off two hours later, flying independently along the southern route. They would serve as a mobile reserve to be allocated as required under direct radio control from No. 5 Group Headquarters at Grantham. Should all three main targets be breached, a number of smaller targets had additionally been designated.

Of the Sorpe wave, Pilot Officer Vernon Byers was shot down over Texel. Pilot Officer Geoff Rice and Flight Lieutenant Munro were forced to return. Rice flew too low over the Zuider Zee, hit the water, which tore off his Upkeep, while Munro was hit by a single 20mm shell as he crossed the Dutch Islands, which damaged his master compass and destroyed his intercom, rendering impossible crew co-operation and execution of attack. Flight Lieutenant Barlow reached Rees, but shortly afterwards flew into high-tension cables, which brought down his Lancaster with the loss of all on board and inadvertently presented the Germans with an intact example of Upkeep.

Forced by mechanical failure at start-up to transfer to the reserve aircraft, Flight Lieutenant Joe McCarthy, an American serving in the RCAF, was alone in reaching the Sorpe. After several attempts, hampered by poor visibility, he released his Upkeep, causing minor crumbling of the crest.

Wing Commander Gibson led his nine aircraft to the Möhne. They ran into small pockets of flak en route, but arrived at the target minus only Flight Lieutenant Bill Astell. At 0025 Gibson made the first attack. It was a good run, but his Upkeep sank and detonated 30 yards from the dam. Having lost the element of surprise, Flight Lieutenant John Hopgood, already damaged on the flight out, came under heavy fire, was set on fire and crashed. His Upkeep overshot the dam and exploded on the powerhouse beyond. Supported by Gibson, Martin made the third run, and was also hit, though not seriously. His Upkeep too failed to strike the target, veering off to explode near the left-hand bank, its blast putting the left tower's gun out of action.

Squadron Leader Melvin Young made the fourth attack, with Gibson and Martin drawing the flak. His mine performed perfectly, detonating in contact with the wall, but the dam held. With Gibson and Young distracting the defences, Flight Lieutenant David Maltby made the fifth attack. As he ran in he thought he saw the crest crumbling, and moved his line slightly to port. His too was a perfect run, and, as his Upkeep detonated, Martin, flying parallel to the airside of the dam, saw the wall collapse and a raging, foaming torrent cascade down the valley inundating all before it.

For a few minutes the VHF was full of jubilant voices, soon silenced by Gibson instructing the three aircraft with their mines to accompany him and Young to the Eder. There they found mist forming, hindering identification of the target. It was eventually found by Gibson, who fired a Very light to attract the others. The Eder had no defences, but was cradled by steep-sided hills, necessitating a dog-leg approach: a steep dive to the lake, turn to port to the release point and a climbing turn to starboard to avoid rising ground beyond the dam.

Squadron Leader Henry Maudslay and Australian Flight Lieutenant David Shannon both attempted runs, but found it extremely demanding in a heavily laden Lancaster. Shannon made a further run, and released his weapon, striking the dam to the right of centre, without effect. After several further attempts, and with Gibson urging the attack to commence, Maudslay released his weapon. The Upkeep struck the dam parapet, detonating just beneath and behind the aircraft, which could be seen banking steeply in the flash from the explosion. After transmitting a brief and faint radio message, suggesting that he had survived but was possibly damaged, Maudslay headed for home. Approaching the Rhine, and slightly off the planned route, he ran into intense light flak defending the port of Emmerich, which brought the Lancaster down, killing all on board.

This now left only Australian Pilot Officer Les Knight. After several abortive attempts, he made a perfect run. His Upkeep bounced three times, striking the target. As he banked and climbed away, his navigator, looking back from the astrodome, saw the tremendous spout as the mine exploded, then a hole appeared, leaving the crest briefly as a bridge before it too crumbled and fell into the maelstrom pounding down the steep Eder Valley.

With the two main targets breached, Gibson and his fellow crews headed back to the Möhne, now difficult to identify since the landscape had changed, before setting course on their own individual routes home. At the last moment, as they crossed the Dutch coast, a final burst of flak would claim the lives of Squadron Leader Young and his crew.

The mobile reserve, by now over Germany, had encountered significant resistance, perhaps alerted by the passage of previous aircraft. Pilot Officer Lewis Burpee ran into trouble when he strayed off track shortly after crossing the Dutch coast and crossed Gilze Rijen airfield. Witness accounts vary, but he was either hit by light flak or dazzled by a searchlight. Out of control, his aircraft crashed, causing significant damage to buildings on the airfield.

Pilot Officer Warner Ottley had just received instructions to attack the Sorpe when his aircraft was raked by light flak. His blazing aircraft crashed near Hamm, killing all except the rear gunner. Flight Sergeant Frank Tees's turret broke away when the aircraft crashed, throwing him clear, bruised and burned, but still alive.

Flight Sergeant Bill Townsend ran into flak east of the Rhine, which he managed to avoid by handling the heavy bomber 'as though it were a Tiger Moth' and flying along a fire break between banks of woodland. The crew could see the German tracer dipping to scythe through the trees as the gunners sought to follow their progress. Townsend attacked what he believed to be his designated target, the Ennepe Dam, although post-war research points to it being another in the area – the Bever. The Upkeep bounced and sank and detonated short of the wall without effect.

Canadian Flight Sergeant Ken Brown was directed to the Sorpe, already damaged by McCarthy's mine. Hampered by mist, he made six runs before eventually releasing his mine. It was seen to detonate close to the target, but the dam still held.

The final aircraft, captained by Flight Sergeant Cyril Anderson, ran into difficulties on reaching Germany. His rear turret malfunctioned and, with compass problems, time running out and no accurate idea of his position, it was impossible for his crew to locate their target, so expediency decreed that they should return home with their Upkeep.

Having journeyed to Grantham to monitor progress of the operation at No. 5 Group Headquarters, Wallis, accompanied by Harris and Cochrane, returned to Scampton to meet the returning crews and listen to their accounts as they were debriefed. Arriving they found the atmosphere one of jubilation and sorrow. The Möhne and Eder Dams had been destroyed, and the Sorpe possibly damaged. Without doubt a severe blow had been struck against Germany's key centres of industrial production. But the price of this success was high.

Of the 19 Lancasters despatched that Sunday evening, only 11 had returned to Scampton. The previous afternoon Barnes Wallis had stood before 133 young, highly trained airmen, each of an age to be one of his sons, explaining the concept of his weapon that they were about to employ. Now 56 were missing – probably all dead. He was not to know that by a miracle 3 would survive to spend the remainder of their war as POWs. It was a grim realization, and he vowed that in future he would do all within his ability to prevent the loss of aircrew lives.

Although specially selected to perform a specific and exceptional operation, those aircrew who participated in Operation Chastise were nonetheless representative of all who served with Bomber Command. Aged between 18 and 35 and from all walks of life, as members of the United Kingdom, Dominions and Commonwealth Air Forces each had committed himself to serving his country. That they did so, right until the end, contributed in no small measure to the final victory. ●

CHAPTER ONE

'ON THE ALTAR OF FREEDOM'

VERNON BYERS

BY STEVE DARLOW

CHISELLED INTO THE WALLS OF THE CLOISTERS AT THE AIR FORCES MEMORIAL AT RUNNYMEDE ARE THE NAMES OF OVER 20,000 AIRMEN AND AIRWOMEN WHO WERE LOST DURING THE SECOND WORLD WAR, FIGHTING IN BRITAIN, NORTH-WESTERN AND CENTRAL EUROPE AND THE EASTERN ATLANTIC. THEY HAVE NO KNOWN GRAVE. PROMINENT ON COOPER'S HILL, OVERLOOKING THE RIVER THAMES, STANDS THE MEMORIAL'S TOWER, FEATURING THREE STONE FIGURES DEPICTING JUSTICE, VICTORY AND COURAGE, LOOKING INWARD, FACING THE CENTRAL PLINTH'S 'THEIR NAME LIVETH FOR EVERMORE'. AT EITHER EDGE OF THE MEMORIAL TOWER CLOISTER, CURVED NAME-LINED PASSAGES LEAD TO NAME-LINED LOOK-OUTS, TAKING IN VIEWS OF WINDSOR AND THE ENDLESS AIR TRAFFIC AT HEATHROW. ON THE WALLS OF THE EASTERN LOOK-OUT, PANEL 175 COMMEMORATES THE NAME OF 23-YEAR-OLD CANADIAN VERNON WILLIAM BYERS, WHO LOST HIS LIFE ON THE NIGHT OF 16/17 MAY 1943, PILOTING AN AVRO LANCASTER OF NO. 617 SQUADRON.

BORN TO FRANK and Ruby Byers on 24 September 1919, in Star City, Saskatchewan, their son Vernon led a very active lifestyle as a young man. Sport was clearly a significant and important aspect of Vernon's life, and he took part in baseball, rugby, hockey and swimming. When he left school Vernon's work life was just as active. When the war in Europe started, Vernon was working on a farm in Pontrilas, Saskatchewan, and in October 1939 he took up duties in 'Elevator Construction' with Harper Construction in Winnipeg. Then early in 1940 Vernon began work as a miner, with the Hudson Bay Mining and Smelting Company, taking up residence in the mining town of Flin Flon, Manitoba.

In March 1941 21-year-old Vernon William Byers put pen to an enrolment form for the Canadian Army and was taken on strength at No. 10 Clearing Depot, his papers recording 'a healthy appearing young man, desirous of transferring for Active Service with the RCAF'. Vernon took this desire to the next level on 8 May 1941, when he enlisted with the Royal Canadian Air Force, in Winnipeg, indicating a clear preference for flying duties. His ultimate ambition was very apparent. Vernon wanted to be a pilot. He wanted to be at the controls. But first he had to negotiate the medical, and there were concerns over his eyesight. The examiner noted he had worn glasses when he was younger. He had a supernumerary nipple. His height was recorded as 5 foot 8½ inches, weight 156 pounds, complexion ruddy, hazel eyes and dark brown hair. The medical report stated 'Good Development', and good hearing. His vision was noted as 'right 20/30', 'left 20/40'. The condition of his mouth and teeth were recorded as 'satisfactory'. In 1934 Vernon had fractured two ribs. The final remarks by the examining consultant noted 'Good type for pilot'. The first hurdle was overcome. He was going to be in the Air Force 'for the duration'.

Initially Vernon was posted to No. 2 Manning Depot, Brandon, as AC2 (Aircrew) Pilot or Observer. On 24 May 1941 he began training at No. 2 Bombing and Gunnery School, Mossbank, and on 27 July 1941 Vernon arrived at No. 4 Initial Training School, Edmonton, his report recording: 'Worked underground in Flin Flon Mines – sturdy – athletic type – keen to be pilot.' From 25 September Vernon's training continued at No. 5 Elementary and Flying Training School, High River. He seemed to be adapting to the physical demands of training, his report recording 'very good, all around pilot', although his ground training remarks were not so glowing, specifying 'below average, difficulty with signals' but going on to say 'sturdy type, slow to learn but reliable. Conduct excellent'.

On 23 November 1941 Vernon arrived at No. 10 Service Flying Training School, Dauphin, and he steadily accumulated flying hours and experience. On 12 January 1942, however, a mistake led to an endorsement of his record: 'While piloting A/C #7885 at 1630 hrs, came in as if to land at No. 1 Relief Field with the wheels of the A/C in the retracted position, for which he received 14 days C.B.' But this was an isolated incident. On 13 March 1942 Vernon Byers received his flying badge, his final report concluding 'a dependable average pilot in all phases of work' and that Vernon was 'conscientious – just average ability'. Frank and Ruby Byers's son had partly fulfilled his ambition – but only partly. When considering his future service flying career Vernon had indicated his 'Pupil's Choice' as 'Fighter', but the recommendation on the final report was 'Bomber'. Vernon's role in the distant European war had been decided. He was going to become part of the escalating air offensive against Germany, one of nearly 10,000 Canadians who played their part and would not be returning.

Following some embarkation leave, from 14 March to 27 March 1942, Vernon crossed the Atlantic to the UK, and arrived at No. 3 Personnel Reception Centre on 13 May 1942. Six weeks later he was at No. 3 Pilots' Advanced Flying Unit, and on 1 September 1942 he arrived at No. 29 Operational Training Unit at RAF North Luffenham, to start the process of forming a crew. Then on 8 December 1942 Vernon transferred to No. 1654 Conversion Unit, operating with Avro Manchesters and Lancasters at RAF Wigsley, to develop and familiarize himself with the workings and characteristics of flying operational aircraft.

While carrying out the latter stages of his training Vernon quite probably gained an indirect first-hand appreciation of the escalation of the bomber offensive. The RAF Bomber Command attack on

Left
Vernon William Byers.
(National Archives of Canada)

Cologne on the night of 30/31 May 1942 had proved a turning point in the strategic air offensive – the first 'thousand-bomber' raid, the RAF bombers attacking, en masse, a specific target, overwhelming the German air and ground defences. Two further thousand-bomber raids were carried out in June. In each case Bomber Command's Commander-in-Chief Sir Arthur Harris called upon the training units to bolster the numbers and maximize the attacks. Such a policy continued into the autumn of 1942. Vernon Byers would not have taken part in these operational sorties but he witnessed colleagues at his respective training units join their main force colleagues in battle. On 10 September eleven aircraft from No. 29 OTU took part in a raid to Düsseldorf and three nights later eight aircraft would take off from North Luffenham for Bremen. On this night Pilot Officer John Leslie 'Les' Munro RNZAF crashed his No. 29 OTU Wellington three minutes after take-off owing to engine failure. There were no casualties. Les would go on to take part in the Dams Raid. On 16/17 January 1943 and 17/18 January No. 1654 Conversion Unit aircraft were detailed for raids to Berlin, with two failing to return from the latter raid, with a total loss of life – fourteen airmen.

For the final months of 1942, and into 1943, Bomber Command expanded its operational capacity in terms of both front-line strength and tactical innovation. Notable was the introduction of the Pathfinder Force – designated squadrons equipped with pyrotechnics to locate and mark targets for main force crews. In addition, many new squadrons were brought to operational readiness, including No. 467 (Australian) Squadron, within No. 5 Group, in November 1942, to which Vernon Byers was posted three months later.

By March 1943 Sir Arthur Harris felt his force was ready to embark upon a sustained attack against Germany, writing in his post-war memoir: 'At long last we were ready and equipped.' Harris would be focusing his force on the industrial spread of the Ruhr, pitting his Command's tactics and his crew's skill and bravery against the concentration and efficiency of the Ruhr ground defences and the enemy nightfighter crews. As Bomber Command

historians Martin Middlebrook and Chris Everitt commented, in respect of the forthcoming offensive: 'The levels of death and destruction were about to mount dramatically.' The forthcoming Operation Chastise, which Harris would describe as 'one incident in the Battle of the Ruhr', would prove no exception.

On the night of 9/10 March 1943 Sergeant Byers carried out his first operational sortie, 'gardening' in the 'Silverthorne' area – mine-laying (code-name 'gardening') being a common approach in respect of introducing new crews to operational flying in hostile skies. Landing at thirty-five minutes past midnight, following a seven-hour flight, the crew reported: 'Mines laid on time and distance run from Arnholt at 2124 from 800 ft. Successful trip nothing to report.'

Two nights later the same crew (Pilot – Sergeant Vernon Byers, Navigator – Pilot Officer James Warner, Bomb Aimer – Sergeant Arthur Whitaker, Flight Engineer – Sergeant Alastair Taylor, Wireless Operator – Sergeant John Wilkinson, Rear Gunner – Sergeant James McDowell, Mid-Upper Gunner – Sergeant Charles Jarvie) was sent to Stuttgart. Twenty miles from the target area the rear turret lost power, McDowell being able to operate it only by hand. Byers was confronted with a stark choice – abort the sortie or carry on and risk, virtually defenceless,

Left Justice, Victory and Courage at the Air Forces Memorial, Runnymede. *(Fighting High)*

Below Vernon Byers – '… reliable, honest and of excellent character. (*National Archives of Canada*)

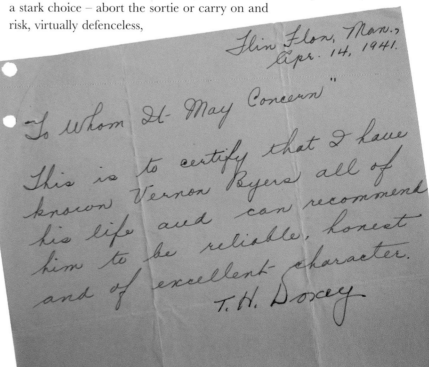

an enemy nightfighter attack from the rear. The crew pressed on, dropping its bombs from 16,000 feet on two green Pathfinder Target Indicators. Landing at 0239 hours, the crew reported: 'Successful effort, one good fire seen going and fairly good concentration of fires.' On 22/23 March the crew carried out what would prove to be its last operational sortie with No. 467 Squadron, to Saint-Nazaire, bombing from 12,000 feet, in what they would record as a 'very concentrated effort'. A few

Right Personal effects of Vernon Byers. *(National Archives of Canada)*

B.10062   Personal Effects of J,17474 P/O. BYERS, V.W.

1. Carton containing:-
6. pair Pyjamas.
1. Pyjama jacket.
3. Pullovers.
1. Scarf.
8. pair Socks.
1. pair Gym shoes.
8. Shirts.
5. Trunks.
3. Vests.
1. Carton containing:-
   Paper and letters. R
2. New Testaments.
3. Cigarette cases.
   Photos.
1. Knife on sheath.
1. Shave kit.
2. Brevets.
1. Hair brush in case.
1. Shave brush.
2. Pipes.
1. Shoe horn.

1. Pencil and Fountain pen.
1. Tooth brush.
1. Belt.
1. Comb.
1. pair Suspenders.
1. pair Braces.
1. Wrist Watch unserviceable
18 Handkerchiefs.
2. Collars.
1. Bottle opener.
   Refill leads.
1. Crested Ronson Lighter.
   Tweezers.
1. Nail file.
   Photo.
2. pair Shoes.
1. pair Slippers.
1. Stud.
1. Dice.
1. Coin.
1. Book.
2. Handkerchiefs.

Next of kin:-

Mr.F.C.Byers (Father)
Pontrillas,
Sask.
Canada.

days later they became part of a new squadron, soon to be designated '617'.

A memo from Headquarters Bomber Command to the AOC No. 5 Group on 17 March 1943 recorded that the operations against the dams would not, 'it is thought, prove particularly dangerous, but will undoubtedly require skilled crews. Volunteer crews will therefore have to be carefully selected from the Squadrons in your Group.'

In such a context it seems remarkable that, on 24 March 1943, Vernon Byers, who had to date carried out two bombing operations from 12,000 and 16,000 feet and a mine-laying operation from a 'low-level' 800 feet, was transferred to No. 617 Squadron. Most of Vernon's crew were similarly inexperienced, although Charles Jarvie and Arthur Whitaker had been with No. 467 Squadron since November 1942. At No. 617 Squadron Byers and his novice colleagues would quickly have to re-appraise their perception of what 'low-level' operational flying could actually entail. As the month of March drew to a close, Sergeant Vernon Byers and his crew embarked upon a sustained period of intense training in order to attack a unique target with one of the most secret weapons developed in the war to date.

A further memo from Headquarters Bomber Command to No. 5 Group a month prior to the Dams Raid outlined future recruitment policy post Chastise, in which No. 617 Squadron's 'duties will consist of performing operations that entail special training and/or the use of special equipment'.

The aircrew personnel for this Squadron should, as far as possible, be recruited from within the Group. [This was changed post-Chastise to all operational Groups.] As the work is not expected to be arduous full use should be made of crews who have completed two operational tours and who apply to take part in further operations. It is not intended that crews at present in this Squadron should be moved, but the future policy should ensure that a high percentage of the aircrew personnel are time expired experienced crews that need a rest from normal operation, but one capable of performing in special tasks that may be allotted to this Squadron.

But such policy was clearly not being applied, in full, in the selection of the original No. 617 Squadron crews. Sergeant Byers was in the early stages of

operational flying and certainly not experienced, and nowhere in his flying record is there comment on any exceptional flying abilities. Nowhere is there evidence of the Byers crew being particularly 'skilled'. Was this crew really appropriate for selection? It is very difficult not to question, in the light of the documentary evidence, the suitability of the Byers crew. However, as training continued it does appear that Byers was impressing CO Gibson. On 17 April 1943 he was recommended for a commission, with

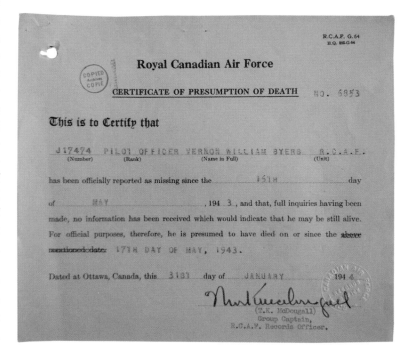

Gibson recording 'A good type of NCO who is fully capable of holding down a commission. He keeps his crew in order, is punctual, and understands discipline. Recommended.' A few days before the Dams Raid Vernon became a Pilot Officer.

Byers's Lancaster, 'AJ-K', was the second to take off, late on the evening of 16 May 1943, part of the five-aircraft first wave detailed to fly a long northerly route to the Sorpe Dam. Barlow led the way, taking off at 2128 hours, Byers at 2130, Rice at 2131, Munro at 2139 and McCarthy at 2201, delayed as a result of having to transfer to a reserve aircraft. The route to target took the wave due east from Scampton, across the North Sea, toward the West Frisian Islands. Prior to reaching landfall at Vlieland, the wave was detailed to make a south-easterly

Most of the sixty-seven Commonwealth burials at Harlingen General Cemetery are airmen of the Second World War. One is that of Vernon Byers' colleague James McDowell. Of the other burials twenty-two are unidentified. *(Fighting High)*

Right
Recommendation
for a note to be added
to personnel records
for those who took
part in Operation.
Chastise. (*National
Archives of Canada*)

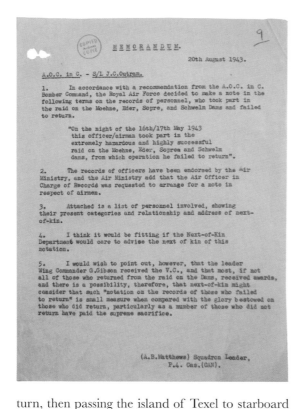

Right The headstone
of air gunner James
McDowell, plot E,
row 4, grave 11,
Harlingen General
Cemetery. Flight
Sergeant McDowell
was the only member
of Vernon Byers'
crew recovered.
(*National Archives of
Canada*)

turn, then passing the island of Texel to starboard and continuing across the Ijsselmeer and on towards Rees and a dog-leg to head east to the target area. But McCarthy's crew would be the only ones to reach the target that night. Flak damage to Munro's aircraft resulted in a loss of communication and he aborted. Flying Officer Rice lost his Upkeep, following contact with the sea, and he returned to Scampton. Barlow and Byers failed to return. Rice's crew reported seeing an aircraft shot down off Texel, and a post-raid summary recorded:

E [Barlow] or K [Byers] is thought to have been shot down from 300 feet off Texel by light flak at 22.57 hrs. If this aircraft was one of the second wave [sic], then; i) it was flying higher that detailed (possibly to obtain a pinpoint on the coast) or ii) it was either off track to the south of the leg from Base or had altered course from the D.R. position 5320–0454E too early so crossing the Texel area west of track.

It was well known, of course, that the West Frisians were a formidable defensive barrier, and timing and accuracy in penetrating these defences at low level were vital. Eventually it became clear that the aircraft shot down into the sea off Texel was indeed Byers's Lancaster. Could its loss be put down to a

lack of operational experience? Or was it simply a case of tragic bad luck – an opportunist lucky strike by a gunner who, it seems, had managed to lower, aim and fire his weapon in what would have been a matter of seconds. Flight Lieutenant Barlow and his crew lost their lives when their aircraft struck an electricity pylon and crashed in flames.

Vernon Byers had failed to return. As had happened thousands of times in the war, the awful news had to be conveyed to a next of kin, initially by telegram, followed by official and personal correspondence.

A letter to Frank Byers from 'Wing Commander, Commanding No. 617 Squadron' expressed deep regret and explained:

Sergeant Byers encountered trouble on the way to the target and contact was lost with him, and nothing more was heard of the aircraft. If, as is possible, your son was able to abandon his aircraft and land safely in enemy territory, news would reach you direct from the International Red Cross Committee within the next six seeks. Please accept my sincere sympathy during this anxious period of waiting.

But no news was forthcoming in the short term. On 11 January 1944 Frank Byers did receive news from

the RCAF Casualties Officer, that the International Red Cross had information concerning Sergeant McDowell and that he had been killed and his body recovered on 22 June 1943. 'I wish to point out that although the Air Ministry now proposes to presume your son's death, it is for official purposes only, and by such action the search being made for him will not be affected or diminished in any way.'

The Royal Canadian Air Force's 'Certificate of Presumption of Death' (No. 6853) was issued on 31 January 1944, recording:

This is to Certify that J17474 Pilot Officer Vernon William Byers R.C.A.F. has been officially reported as missing since the 16th day of May 1943, and that, full inquiries having been made, no information has been received which would indicate that he may be still alive. For official purposes, therefore, he is presumed to have died on or since the 17th Day of May, 1943.

Vernon Byers was one of fifty-six men who had not returned from the Dams Raid. He was one of fifty-three men who had lost their lives. Those who returned received the accolades they justly deserved, but what of those who had been killed or who became prisoners. Sir Arthur Harris made a recommendation of wording that should appear in the records of personnel who took part in the raid and who failed to return. In accordance with this, Vernon's service records show, 'On the night of 16/17.5.43 this airman (now officer) took part in the extremely hazardous and highly successful raid on the Moehne, Eder, Sorpe and Schwelm dams, from which he failed to return.' A note from Harris in the official files also records: 'I think it would be fitting if the Next-of-Kin Department would care to advise the next of kin of this notation.' It went on:

I would wish to point out, however, that the leader Wing Commander G. Gibson received the V.C., and that most, if not all of those who returned from the raid on the Dams, received awards, and there is a possibility, therefore, that next-of-kin might consider that such 'notation on the records of those who failed to return' is small measure when compared with the glory on those who did return, particularly as a number of those who did not return have paid the supreme sacrifice.

Two and a half years after receiving his son's

Their Name Liveth For Evermore, Air Forces Memorial, Runnymede. Included among the names of the missing are:
P/O Vernon Byers
Sgt Alastair Taylor
F/O James Warner
P/O Arthur Whitaker
Sgt John Wilkinson
Sgt Charles Jarvie.
(Fighting High)

'Certificate of Presumption of Death' Frank Byers, on 15 August 1946, received a package containing a letter.

It is a privilege to have the opportunity of sending you the Operational Wings and Certificate in recognition of the gallant services rendered by your son Pilot Officer V. W. Byers. I realize there is little which may be said or done to lessen your sorrow but it is my hope that these 'Wings', indicative of operations against the enemy, will be a treasured memento of a young life offered on the altar of freedom in defence of his Home and Country.

A further two and half years passed before a final memorandum was added to Vernon's file, stating that the burial place of Flight Sergeant McDowell was recorded as Harlingen General Cemetery, along with the comment: 'As the body of F/S McDowell was washed ashore off the Coast of Holland it is assumed that the aircraft was shot down over the sea. Classified. Lost at Sea. Case Closed.' ●

CHAPTER TWO

'HAPPY HE WHOSE COURSE IS SPED'

BILL ASTELL, DFC

BY ROBERT OWEN

ONLY ONE AIRCRAFT FROM THE MAIN FORCE OF NINE AIRCRAFT DETAILED TO ATTACK THE MÖHNE AND EDER DAMS FAILED TO REACH ITS TARGET. ED864 AJ-B WAS FLOWN BY BILL ASTELL, A PILOT WHO HAD SURVIVED A NUMBER OF INCIDENTS FLYING WELLINGTONS IN THE MIDDLE EAST. CONTEMPORARIES RECALL HIM AS ONE OF THE MOST GALLANT AND INSPIRING PILOTS IN BOMBER COMMAND, COMBINING PROFESSIONALISM AND DEDICATION TO DUTY WITH A SUPERB SENSE OF HUMOUR, FULL OF FUN, A CHEERFUL SMILE ON HIS FACE FREQUENTLY PUNCTUATED BY HIS PIPE, LIFTING THE SPIRITS OF THOSE AROUND HIM.

WILLIAM ASTELL WAS born in Peover, Knutsford, on 1 April 1920, the son of Godfrey Grant Astell and Margery Helen Astell. His father's position as Managing Director of Manchester textile manufacturer J. and N. Philips provided Bill with a comfortable and advantaged childhood. After initial schooling at Abberley Hall, Worcester, and Aysgarth School, Yorkshire, he was sent in 1933 to complete his education at Bradfield College, Berkshire. While there, he developed a sense for adventure and the sea. Returning in September 1935, he travelled from Manchester to London by tramp steamer, arriving two days late owing to a gale, and the following summer he crossed the Atlantic by cargo boat to visit relatives in Canada. On leaving school in September 1937 he boarded a trawler for a voyage to the White Sea, en route to a position with a German glove manufacturing company at Burgstadt in Saxony, where he would hone his language skills and gain commercial experience in preparation for work in his father's company. While there he spent three months at Leipzig University, and then, spending July 1938 climbing in the Dolomites, moved on to Paris and Nice, returning to England in May 1939.

Sensing the threat of war, Bill had enlisted in the RNVR, but his father had found him a position at Philips' Tean Hall Mill at Tean, Staffordshire, which made it impossible for him to attend the requisite training sessions at the Liverpool Training Ship. The presence of an airfield a few miles away at Meir provided the incentive for his transfer to the RAFVR, and his training commenced there after enlisting on 5 July 1939. After a few months he was mobilized and left Staffordshire for No. 5 Initial Training Wing at Hastings. There he learned basic military discipline and elements of airmanship, which confirmed that he would be one of ten on his course selected for pilot training in southern Africa. Thus in April 1940 Bill found himself at sea again, sailing from Southampton in a grey-painted Union-Castle vessel, on a two-week voyage bound for Cape Town. Sailing alone, rather than in convoy, and zigzagging to avoid U-boats, this was 'a pretty old ship and shakes a good deal'. Sharing a cabin with three others and with the cabin blacked out at night, in an effort to keep cool he borrowed a

hammock to sling on the boat deck as the vessel entered tropical climes. There was little to do except read, play bridge and run round the decks for exercise. Calling in to re-fuel at Dakar, 'quite the foulest place on earth', the vessel collided with the quayside, springing bow plates; the remainder of the journey was completed with one compart-ment flooded. As they neared their destination on 11 May, Bill sleeping on deck was able to observe the sunrise over Table Mountain. After docking they were transferred immediately to a train for a hot and dusty three-day journey to Salisbury, Rhodesia (now Harare, Zimbabwe).

Accommodated in a tin hut at No. 1 Elementary Flying Training School, Belvedere Camp, with a native boy as a servant, Bill was soon using family and business contacts to establish a new social circle, enjoying sailing, tennis, hockey and shooting kudu and sable in off-duty hours. But already the realities of war were beginning to register, as he found himself combing the casualty lists and find-ing friends' names. A period of ground instruction and further ab initio training was followed by transfer to No. 20 Flying Training School at Cran-bourne, on the other side of Salisbury, to begin his intermediate training on Airspeed Oxfords: 'So I am pretty certain to be put onto bombers, which is what I always wanted.' On 21 August he completed his first solo cross-country and by late October had commenced practice bombing and firing 'with queer results at times'. A week later the course was over. On 2 November he was awarded his flying badge and commissioned as an officer the following day. Unable to obtain a new uniform, he simply sewed epaulettes on to his sergeant's tunic.

Any hopes that he might be posted back to the UK were dashed when two days later he found he was to be transferred to No. 70 Operational Training Unit, training aircrew for the Middle East. Board-ing a train, he travelled to Durban to await a ship to take him north. He found Durban quiet, 'not a lot to do . . . [but] there is a very good country club where we played squash and tennis, but there was not a lot else to do except bathe'. The tedium was

further broken when he managed to accompany a South African Air Force pilot on an early morning anti-submarine patrol.

He sailed north aboard a former Dutch liner, the *Westernland*, but his arrival at Ismalia was not quite what he expected. It was cold. There was no wood or coal for the Mess fire, so he wore his blue serge to keep warm. Continuous sand-storms covered everything with dust; 'the Mess billiard table is in a very bad way indeed'. The OTU operated Blenheims, which kept his spirits up, as he hoped to be posted to a Blenheim squadron. At last, his next posting was confirmed, to No. 148 Squadron – flying Wellington Ics.

No. 148 Squadron was based at Luqa, on the be-leaguered island of Malta. Arriving on 31 January, Bill found himself allocated to 'B' Flight. Since his only twin-engined experience was on Oxfords, he would be assigned initially for second pilot duties with Pilot Officer Cowan and crew. Bill found Malta 'not much of a place, thousands of stone walls and not a field bigger than the lawn at home'. Air raids nearly every day did little to improve the bleakness of the landscape. He was living on rations in the

Mess, and it was not long until he fell victim to the island's overburdened and battered water supply, contracting typhoid, which necessitated a lengthy stay in hospital, including his twenty-first birthday. A period of enforced convalescence, 'bathing and sailing' lasted until the end of April, by which time No. 148 Squadron had left the island and was now based at Kabrit, Egypt, providing support for the 8th Army in the desert.

Bill caught up with the squadron in the middle of May. Finding that accommodation was at a premium, he camped out in a tent – but there was a camp cinema, a concrete cricket pitch and swimming in the Great Bitter Lake. More permanent quarters were eventually found: 'I have been trying to get my room squared up a bit. Now I am such an expert carpenter that I could easily make a set of Chippendale chairs with the assistance of a hammer and a few petrol boxes.' However, there was another job to do, and he set about concluding his conversion to the Wellington, operating with Pilot Officer Cowan. In June he completed a night landing course – an essential prerequisite to becoming a captain. By July he had his own crew, but not for operations, initially flying air tests, taking spares to an advanced base and conducting air–sea rescue searches. It was essential but uninspiring work. Thirsting for more action, he wrote home towards the end of the month: 'Thinking of transferring to Blenheims or something a bit smaller, they see more of the fun than we do at present.'

By September the squadron had received a number of Merlin-engined Wellington IIs, capable of accommodating a 4,000-pounder, and all pilots were instructed to do an hour's night flying, three hours' cross-country to test fuel and oil consumption, and three night landings. The resting of a number of operationally expired pilots finally gave Bill the chance to become a captain with his own crew, and on 28 September he departed to advanced Landing Ground Z prior to an uneventful operation against the Libyan enemy supply port of Bardia. From now on, interrupted only by a minor bout of jaundice, life would settle down to a regular routine of flights from Kabrit to a forward operating base – a desert airstrip with rudimentary facilities for servicing and refuelling – followed by take-off for the target, usually a port, supply base

or airfield, with recovery to the advanced base to refuel before returning to Kabrit. Such was the regularity of these trips to targets such as Benghazi that they became known as 'the Mail Run'. During the night of 29 November his observer, Sergeant Geary, a veteran on his 73rd operation, his third with Bill, claimed a direct hit on a vessel in the harbour, and was recommended for an immediate DFM.

On 4 December Bill's father received a telegram: 'Regret to inform you that your son Pilot Officer William Astell is reported suffering from scalp wounds and facial injuries as a result of an aircraft accident on 30 November 1941 and admitted to No. 19 General Hospital, Middle East. Any further information will be immediately communicated to you.'

Returning from an operation against Benghazi on the night of 30 November/1 December, Bill had been given permission to land at LG 60, but, unobserved, a No. 37 Squadron aircraft cut in ahead of him, landed and remained on the runway. Bill saw the obstruction only as he was about to touch down and tried to go round again, but stalled. In his own words, 'up she went and down she came', the port wing hitting the ground, tearing off at the root, swinging the aircraft round. The wreckage burst into flame, but the crew managed to escape with varying degrees of injury save for the rear gunner who was unhurt. Bill had cracked his head, fracturing his skull, requiring thirty-two stitches to seal a wound running from above his left eye to behind the ear and suffered second-degree burns to the small of his back. 'As I stepped from the wreckage a tongue of flame caught me on the posterior.'

After remedial treatment the crew was flown back at full speed to Kabrit for specialist care. As he came round from the anaesthetic, Bill was reported to murmur: 'What we do for 14/6 [73p] a day.' He was allowed up for the first time on Christmas Eve

Below A pensive Bill Astell, showing the injury received following his collision with another aircraft during landing. *(Author's collection)*

Right Herman
Goering and Adolf
Hitler observe the
crew's work. A
certificate recording
the crew's accuracy
during an operation
against Lorient,
16 February 1943.
(Author's collection)

and was soon walking to the other end of the camp
and back, before boredom and frustration set in:
'Nothing to do except walk round the desert and
read books.' Having suffered concussion, Bill was
granted three months' sick leave, and on 30 January
1942 he proceeded to Kenya aboard a flying boat
with ten other operationally expired pilots. He
passed the time at a friend's farm near Nakuru. It
was refreshing to see vegetation rather than the
relentless sand, and to go riding, bird shooting; on
one occasion he shot a leopard that had ventured
into the garden.

He returned to the squadron in the middle of
March, 'after a rather stormy session with a
psychiatrist who eventually decided that I was
normal', to find that he had been allocated a new
crew, 'completely new to the game, but very charm-
ing and I am sure we will get on well'. After a
couple of attempts to operate, thwarted by a burst
hydraulic pipe and the weather, the crew restarted
operations on Bill's birthday. Things had not
changed. The target that night was Benghazi. The
end of April saw a trip back to Malta, from where
they planned to attack Messina, but the operation
was cancelled. Engine trouble forced them to
abandon their initial attempt to return to Egypt,
but this was accomplished safely after rectifications
had been effected. More operations to Benghazi were
interspersed with air tests. On 13 May, investigating
fuel consumption, he flew down over the edge of
the Qattara Depression and continued the sortie
with some spirited flying below sea level. He was
now used to the desert life out at LG 106; there was
bathing in the sea, the sound of a nearby railway
reminded him of home, and he was becoming adept
at creating home comforts out of sandbags, petrol
tins and bomb boxes.

But things were about to change. On the night
of 30 May 1942 (while bomber crews in Europe
were taking part in the first thousand-bomber raid
against Cologne), Bill was detailed for an attack
against an enemy airfield at Derna. Making his first
bombing run shortly after midnight, he was circling
at about 3,000 feet for a second run when a burst of
tracer from a nightfighter ripped through the aircraft, putting the rear turret out of action, severing
the rudder controls and starting a fire in the
fuselage. Bill immediately jettisoned the bombs and

headed for home. Two minutes later the fighter
made a second attack, setting fire to the starboard
wing and rear turret ammunition and wounding
the second pilot and wireless operator. Unable to
maintain height, Bill ordered the crew to bale out,
during which time the fighter made a third attack,
cannon shells wrecking the instrument panel. The
rear of the aircraft and wing were now well ablaze,
but it was too late for Bill and his navigator, Pilot
Officer Arthur 'Bishop' Dodds (a clergyman's son),
to leave. Exercising great skill, and with luck on his
side, Bill managed to execute a successful crash
landing 1½ miles south of an enemy airfield at
Martuba, which was being attacked. Bill and 'Bish'
were uninjured and, after quickly destroying documents and equipment, they gathered together maps,
two water bottles, escape compass and revolver,
before fleeing from the blazing wreck, which exploded after they had run 80 yards. Estimating that
they were 120 miles behind enemy lines, they set off
across the desert. After about 8 miles they took
shelter in a cave as dawn broke. The second night
their water ran out and on the third night, almost
exhausted, they came across the sleeping crew of a
German anti-tank gun. They managed to steal an

onion and tin of red peppers, and shortly afterwards came across a tent with a water container, which they used to fill their bottles. Hiding up the next day in a nearby bush, that night they refilled their bottles and took the container with them. They were now approaching the battle zone and saw much German activity. On 5 June they hid in a Wadi that was being shelled by both sides. They were weak and emaciated, Bill's skin stretched taught across his drawn face like parchment. Moving on that night, they circumvented further German positions, at one point finding themselves among German wiring parties. On being challenged, Bill, with great presence of mind, replied in perfect German, 'We are signallers.' They were allowed to proceed. A vehicle approached, firing at the wiring party. Bill set off towards it, firing the revolver, hoping to attract the crew's attention, but to no avail. Returning to where he thought he had left Dodds, he was unable to find him, and headed onward alone towards Allied lines, where, after walking through a supposedly mined area, he was challenged by a member of the Rand Light infantry. His identity verified, the South Africans sent a party in search of Dodds, but he had already been captured by Italian troops. Evacuated via Gazala and Tobruk, Bill returned to Kabrit five days overdue, qualifying him for membership of the 'Late Arrivals Club' and its unofficial badge of a winged flying boot.

Officialdom would recognize his achievement with the award of the DFC, and also determined that Bill's time in the desert was over. By 13 June he was in Cairo waiting for a boat home. His return journey would take him to Canada, where he had the opportunity to visit his uncle in Ontario, and a holiday camp in Maine. Thence his first attempt to return to the UK was thwarted when a US escort vessel collided with the troopship and he had to return to await a crossing on the *Queen Mary*, arriving back in mid-September.

Although an accomplished and skilful pilot, Bill had no experience of operations over western Europe, and it was intended that he would spend an initial period as an instructor, but he first had to become proficient with the latest types being introduced into Bomber Command. To this end he was posted to No. 1654 Conversion Unit at Wigsley,

Nottinghamshire, which was equipped with the Avro Manchester and Lancaster. Arriving on 4 October, Bill considered them 'simply enormous machines', and he still found the sight of ploughed fields strange after so much sand. Having learned the rudiments, he was sent on a short course to the Flying Instructors' School at Hullavington, after which, on 3 December, in typical contrary fashion, he found himself posted to No. 1485 Bombing and Gunnery Flight at Fulbeck, flying Manchesters for trainee air gunners. It was to be a brief sojourn, and on 25 January 1943 he was instructed to report to No. 57 Squadron at RAF Scampton.

After a brief refresher course with 1506 BAT Flight at Waddington, he was ready to commence his second operational tour. Rather than experiencing a familiarization trip as 'second dickey' with an experienced crew, Bill immediately captained his newly formed Lancaster crew on an operation against the French port of Lorient on 13/14 February. It was a revealing induction, being the first time that over 1,000 tons of bombs had been

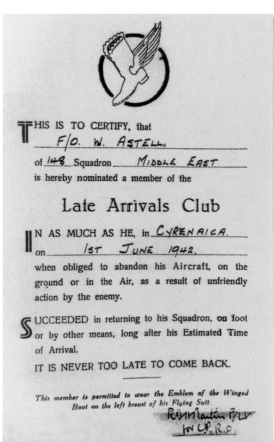

Left 'Order of the Winged Flying Boot'; Bill's certificate confirming his membership of the 'Late Arrivals Club'. *(Author's collection)*

Below
An inner engine nacelle, outer wing panel and propeller lie among the burned-out remains of ED864 AJ-B at Marbeck, 17 May 1943. *(R. Hepner)*

The remains of the tail section of ED864 AJ-B on the morning of 17 May 1943. *(R. Hepner)*

dropped during an attack on a target in occupied territory. The crew did not see the effect of their 4,000-pounder and incendiaries, which were swallowed by the huge fires already blazing below. During the next six weeks the crew would complete many operations against targets that were familiar during this stage of the war, a long haul over the Alps to Milan and penetrations into Germany including Bremen, Nuremberg and Essen, the latter marking the opening of what was to become known as 'the Battle of the Ruhr'. During an operation against Lorient on 16/17 February, an engine was damaged by flak. Technical problems caused Bill to abort two trips, to Hamburg and Berlin, jettisoning his bombs and returning to base. On 22 February he was promoted to Flight Lieutenant, but then suddenly, on 25 March, news came through that No. 57 Squadron's entire 'C' Flight

was being transferred to a new squadron being formed in Scampton's No. 2 Hangar.

The new squadron, shortly to be numbered 617, had few aircraft and was using much borrowed equipment, but there appeared to be a degree of urgency about seemingly non-urgent tasks. On 27 March Bill had the distinction of making the new squadron's first flight, a cross-country, photographing lakes en route. The next few weeks were passed off as a working-up routine, but it soon became clear that this was training for a specific purpose, and that it would be far from routine. In keeping with the other crews Bill was tasked with navigational cross-countries at increasingly lower heights, combined with low-level bombing. When the aircraft modified to carry Upkeep began to arrive, the first was allocated to Bill, rather than to the squadron or flight commanders. The required techniques seemed to come naturally to him, and there appear to have been no untoward incidents. Long cross-countries gave way to those linking Derwent, Uppingham and Abberton reservoirs, as training took on a more tactical nature. Bill does not appear to have dropped an Upkeep himself during the mid-May practices at Reculver, experiencing instead its effects flying as a passenger with Squadron Leader Young on 12 May.

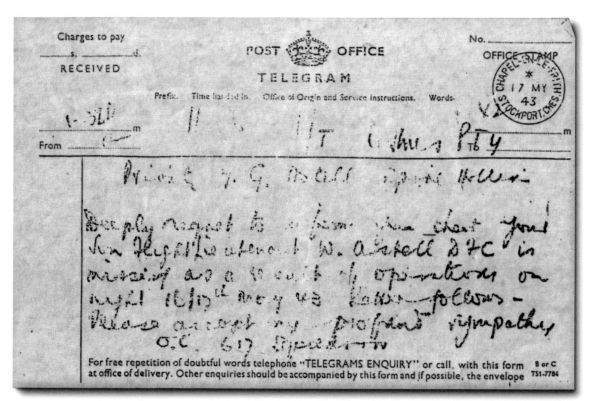

Despite the intensity of training, there were still those off-duty moments. In late March he found himself invited to tour a Lincoln factory, accompanied by the Mayor. Seated on a rudimentary stage in the works canteen, Bill was suddenly aware of his name being mentioned as the Mayor completed his speech and sat down. It was only when someone prodded him and motioned him to the microphone that he realized he was required to speak. 'So I stood up and spoke furthermore I continued to speak until I felt someone pulling at my jacket – then I sat down again. Quite one of the most alarming affairs yet, and to this day I have not the least idea what I said.' At the beginning of April he went to see the film *Random Harvest* and a fortnight later took in the architecture of Lincoln Cathedral, guided by a friend from 57 Squadron. There was time to improve his squash, or lie on the grass observing the habits of partridges sharing his aircraft's dispersal. His membership of the RAF Club was finally ratified, but he would never sample its atmosphere.

On 14 May, those captains who had not yet made a will were instructed to do so. Bill left all to his father, his will being witnessed by two others whose days also were now numbered, Flight Lieutenant Robert Barlow and Squadron Leader Henry Maudslay. The accompanying letter – 'The RAF does take some funny ideas . . .' – suggests a levity that belied a growing awareness that the operation was close. Such atmosphere was still apparent on the evening of 16 May, when, arriving at their aircraft, Sergeant Abram Garshowitz, the Canadian wireless operator, would chalk on their Upkeep: 'Never has so much been asked of so few.'

Bill was part of the third formation of the main force of nine aircraft detailed to attack the Möhne and Eder Dams. Taking off at 2159 along with Pilot Officer Les Knight and led by Squadron Leader Henry Maudslay, the aircraft were to fly the southern route into Holland. All seems to have gone well until 2352 hours, when they reached the T-shaped canal junction at Beek, where they would turn north-east to take them to the Rhine near Rees and then skirt round the northern defences of the Ruhr. At this point the formation appears to have broken up, with the result that Bill's aircraft dropped behind before assuming the correct course. Shortly after crossing the Rhine the formation was further fragmented as they ran into unexpected light flak. The

The pylon struck by Bill Astell's Lancaster ED864 AJ-B causing it to crash in the field beyond the farmhouse. *(Fighting High)*

Memorial stone erected by Raesfeld Museum marking the field where Bill Astell's seven-man crew died. *(Fighting High)*

vic formation was now flying in an extended line astern, Maudslay leading, followed by Knight, with Bill trailing at the rear.

The community of Marbeck lies midway between the towns of Raesfeld and Borken and some 9 miles north of the industrial Ruhr conurbation. It comprises a number of scattered farms and rural dwellings and lay right in the path of the approaching Lancasters. Despite the proximity of this area to the Ruhr, the relatively flat countryside, comprising a mixture of fields and woodland, was somewhat free of defences other than a searchlight position on the outskirts of Raesfeld. In theory this should have afforded a clear run to the approaching aircraft, save for one potential danger. Crossing the area, running diagonally from south-west to north-east, lay a line of high-tension cables supported on tall, slender pylons. Witnesses on the ground heard Gibson's and Young's waves pass over in formation, flying so low that it was thought that they must be Luftwaffe aircraft. Some ten minutes later, at about a quarter past midnight, more aircraft were heard. Two had passed overhead, receding to the east when about a minute later a third approached. There was a loud noise, and the sky was lit by a flash and a burst of flame.

The third machine was Bill's Lancaster. Flying at treetop height, it had struck the top of a pylon supporting the cables across a field some 220 yards west of the farm occupied by the Thesing family. The impact had dislodged the upper section of the pylon and ripped into the aircraft. The extent of the damage can only be speculation, but it was to prove fatal. The aircraft caught fire almost immediately and rose slightly, possibly the result of the pilot having seen the obstruction at the last moment and desperately trying to hurdle the mast, or as a result of the impact. It skimmed over the roofs of the Thesing's farm, travelling some 650 yards beyond the pylon to crash in a field to the north-east of an adjacent crossroads, disintegrating on impact. Its Upkeep, covered in blazing fuel and oil, continued travelling for a further 100 yards or so. Some ninety seconds later there was a further tremendous explosion as the weapon's 6,600 lb of RDX detonated, triggered by the self-destruct pistol initiated as the mine broke free from the aircraft. Reports suggest that the force of the blast was detected up to a radius of 3 kilometres, with the blast lifting tiles, breaking windows and depositing a layer of dust and soil.

For half an hour rounds of ammunition continued to explode in the heat, and, when the occupants from neighbouring farms were able to approach the burning wreckage, it was clear that none of the crew had survived. All they could do was to assess the damage to their own property and check on livestock. Daylight brought a gathering of observers both local and official, including a photographer from Raesfeld, who photographed the aircraft remains before the bodies of the crew had been recovered. His photographs provide strong testimony to what was only too often the stark reality behind the sanitized phrase 'one of our

Below
Telegram confirming information received from Germany concerning the death of F/Lt William Astell. *(R. Hepner)*

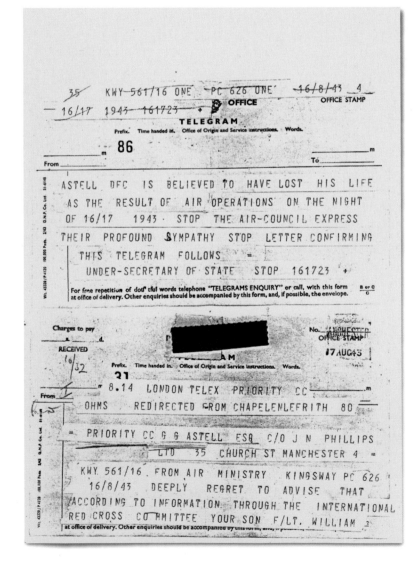

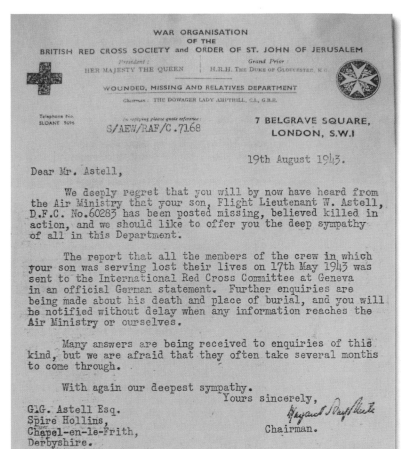

WAR ORGANISATION
OF THE
BRITISH RED CROSS SOCIETY and ORDER OF ST. JOHN OF JERUSALEM

President : HER MAJESTY THE QUEEN | *Grand Prior :* H.R.H. The DUKE OF GLOUCESTER, K.G.

WOUNDED, MISSING AND RELATIVES DEPARTMENT

Chairman : THE DOWAGER LADY AMPTHILL, C.I., G.B.E.

Telephone No. SLOANE 9496

In replying please quote reference : S/AEW/RAF/C.7168

7 BELGRAVE SQUARE,
LONDON, S.W.1

19th August 1943.

Dear Mr. Astell,

We deeply regret that you will by now have heard from the Air Ministry that your son, Flight Lieutenant W. Astell, D.F.C. No.60283 has been posted missing, believed killed in action, and we should like to offer you the deep sympathy of all in this Department.

The report that all the members of the crew in which your son was serving lost their lives on 17th May 1943 was sent to the International Red Cross Committee at Geneva in an official German statement. Further enquiries are being made about his death and place of burial, and you will be notified without delay when any information reaches the Air Ministry or ourselves.

Many answers are being received to enquiries of this kind, but we are afraid that they often take several months to come through.

With again our deepest sympathy.

Yours sincerely,

G.G. Astell Esq.
Spire Hollins,
Chapel-en-le-Frith,
Derbyshire.

Chairman.

aircraft is missing'. Close by, a roadside shrine to St Joseph watched over the scene, miraculously unharmed by the explosion. By strange coincidence, while struggling to develop Upkeep, an associate had sent Wallis a prayer of supplication to the self-same saint.

The bodies of the crew were taken to Borken, where they were laid to rest in the City Cemetery. Meanwhile, back at Scampton, Flight Lieutenant Harry Humphries, the Squadron Adjutant, was despatching the standard casualty telegram to Mr and Mrs Astell at Spire Hollins, Combs, near Chapel-en-le-Frith: 'Your son . . . is missing as the result of operations.' A period of protracted suspense followed, hope tempered with despair as the days passed without news. Then, on 17 August, followed three days later by a confirmatory letter from the Air Ministry Casualty Branch dispelling all doubt, came the news they dreaded: 'Quoting official German information . . . your son and six other occupants of the aircraft in which he was

flying . . . were killed on the 17th May.'

Bill Astell and the other members of his crew were reinterred in the Commonwealth War Graves Cemetery at Reichswald in 1948, the following inscription being requested by his parents in final tribute:

Think not of me as dead:
Happy he whose course is sped.
He has gone home to God. ●

Hier starb die Besatzung des "DAMBUSTER"-Fluges:
Here died the "DAMBUSTER" crew of:

617 Sqn. LANCASTER ED864 AJ-B
16th May, 1943

Pilot-Flight Lieutenant W. ASTELL DFC
Navigator-Pilot Officer F. A. WILE
Flight Engineer-Sergeant J. KINNEAR
Bomb Aimer-Flying Officer D. HOPKINSON
Wireless Operator-Warrant Officer A. A. GARSHOWITZ
Front Gunner-Flight Sergeant F. A. GARBAS
Rear Gunner-Sergeant R. BOLITHO

HEIMATVEREIN RAESFELD. 2003.

Above left
This statue to St Joseph originally stood as a roadside shrine adjacent to the crash site of AJ-B. *(Author's collection)*

Above
The Red Cross letter confirming the earlier telegram reporting F/Lt Astell's death. *(R. Hepner)*

Left Close-up of the panel on the memorial stone marking the crash site of Bill Astell's Lancaster. *(Author's collection)*

Twenty-three year-old
Bill Astell, DFC, rests
with his colleagues at
the Reichswald Forest
War Cemetery.
(Fighting High)

CHAPTER THREE

MOTHER'S LOVE

TONY BURCHER, DFM AND JOHN FRASER

BY SEAN FEAST

OF THE THREE SURVIVORS FROM THE DAMS RAID WHO 'FAILED TO RETURN', TWO WERE FROM THE SAME CREW: THE CREW OF M-MOTHER. THEY BOTH LIVED, WHEN THE ODDS STACKED AGAINST THEIR SURVIVAL WERE OVERWHELMING. AND THEY BOTH LIVED THANKS TO THE OUTSTANDING BRAVERY OF THEIR SKIPPER, WHO PERFORMED AN ACT OF COURAGE THAT MIGHT HAVE EARNED HIGHER REWARD.

O F ALL THE personalities who took part in the Dams Raid, Tony Burcher is undoubtedly one of the most colourful and controversial. He was also one of the most complex.

Born on 15 March 1922, in Vaucluse, an eastern suburb of Sydney, New South Wales, Tony was the fifth of no fewer than twelve children of Harvey and Estelle, described in the quaint language of the time as being Australians of pure European descent. A steady if unspectacular school career was punctuated by greater success on the sports field and on water, as Tony captained the local rugby league team and won various local swimming and sailing championships.

Since his father was a retired grazier, it was perhaps not surprising that Tony followed him into the world of sheep and cattle, and earned a place as a student at Wagga Experimental Farm, where he was studying when war was declared. Having gained his farm certificate, Tony took a variety of jobs as a grazier and wool sorter, and at the first opportunity (in February 1940) volunteered to join the Royal Australian Air Force (RAAF), having reached the age of majority. Indeed, Tony was so impatient to train as aircrew that he wrote to the authorities the following month to ask if his application had been lost!

It was not until July that Tony was finally enrolled in the Reserve at the No. 2 Recruiting Centre at Woolloomooloo. Passing the necessary test to serve as aircrew, and having satisfied the authorities that he had no police record and was not a member of the Communist Party, he was placed on a waiting list, awaiting his place to train. Although he was physically fit, the 18-year-old's personality was described as 'not very impressive'; while his first choice for service was as a pilot – like almost every youngster at that time – the interview board recommended he train as a wireless telegraphist/air gunner (abbreviated on the official paperwork to W/T AG).

Tony formally enlisted on 11 December 1940, 'for the duration of the war and a period of 12 months thereafter', and, after initial training at Bradfield Park, embarked for No. 3 Wireless School in Winnipeg, to train as a wireless operator (W/Op) with the Royal Canadian Air Force (RCAF). He spent four months in Winnipeg before moving to No. 1 Bombing and Air Gunnery School (RAAF) in Jarvis, Ontario, to complete an air gunnery course. It was in October 1941 that he finally arrived in the UK, undertaking a wireless refresher course at No. 2 Signals School, Yatesbury, before moving to No. 14 Operational Training Unit (OTU) in Cottesmore. He was five months at OTU before eventually receiving his first operational posting: No. 106 Squadron, RAF Coningsby.

While Tony Burcher was arriving in England to start the second half of his training, Canadian John Fraser was on his way to Edmonton, to begin his observers' course at No. 2 Air Observers' School (2AOS).

John was only seven months younger than Tony, having been born on 22 September 1922 in Nanaimo, British Columbia. John's father, William, had served in the trenches as an officer in the

Far left John Fraser. *(Shere Fraser McCarthy)*
Left Tony Burcher wearing the ribbon of the DFM under his air gunner's brevet. *(Shere Fraser McCarthy)*

Left John on the day of his wedding to Doris – 29 April, 1943. A short honeymoon was followed by a long incarceration as a prisoner of war. *(Shere Fraser McCarthy)*

Canadian Army and was considerably older than his mother. It was not a surprise, therefore, that William died before John had reached his teenage years, leaving the young boy to care for his mother and four sisters. He took odd jobs around the neighbourhood to make ends meet and, although he was passionate about his sport and the outdoor life, he excelled in the classroom, particularly in maths, his headmaster describing him as 'the cleverest boy he'd ever taught'.

A desire to go to university was thwarted through lack of money rather than ability, and instead John took a job at a sawmill in Port Alberni. With the outbreak of war, John enlisted, on 20 May 1941, having been suitably attested and recommended for pilot training. From No. 2 Manning Depot (2MD), Brandon, he moved straight to No. 4 Service Flying Training School (4SFTS) in Saskatoon, Saskatchewan, but was soon after remustered as an observer. Quite what happened is not clear, for it appears John got partway through his pilot training (he had at least fifteen hours to his name) before a medical examination suggested his eyesight was not quite up to the mark. Although he had 20:20 vision, the muscular action of the two eyes lacked co-ordination. Notwithstanding the excitement and occasional dangers of flying, it was a setback to a discipline that he was clearly enjoying, as evidenced by his many letters home. One, dated 30 June 1941, is typical of many:

I have been up for six and a half hours now – nothing to it – just like riding in an empty truck – lots of fun when they do loops and rolls – stomach feels as if it is in the bottom of the seat – pilots are not supposed to do aerobatics in these planes but they do them.

Saturday night when we came back from Varsery (an auxiliary field) we hedgehopped all the way back – about 150 ft from the ground – scared all the cows and horses on the farms. Friday, another fellow, Hubbert and I went down to Osler (another auxiliary field) to guard a crash there – one engine was laying about 40 ft from the plane – landing gear was smashed – the tail wheel was off and half of one wing – the plane was considered a total wreck, but nobody was hurt. There were three other crashes that day – nobody hurt though.

From 4SFTS John was posted to No. 4 Initial Training School (4ITS) for ten weeks of intensive

Left
John at home with his mother and two sisters. John would write frequently to his family during his long absence overseas.
(Shere Fraser McCarthy)

study in maths, map reading and Air Force law as well as a host of other related subjects. He obtained 98 per cent in his mathematics exam, and overall finished ninth out of a class of 146. Described as 'NCO material' by his commanding officer, LAC Fraser passed on to 2AOS, where he spent three months and finished 6th out of 20. He was not yet deemed suitable for a commission, the Chief Instructor describing him as 'moody'.

A further two months were passed at Bombing and Gunnery School (8 B&GS in Lethbridge), learning the range of skills then expected to earn him his observer brevet (the role was later separated into the dedicated 'navigator' and 'air bomber' categories).

His navigation skills, specifically, were honed still further at No. 1 Air Navigation School (ANS) at RCAF Station Rivers, Manitoba, where he learned the art of astronomical navigation, using the stars and moon for guidance. Assessed as 'average', John concluded his training by finishing 5th in his class of 20 and with a mark of 379 out of a maximum 500, before finally embarking from Halifax for the long and potentially treacherous voyage across the Atlantic to the UK. He arrived in April 1942, much at the same time that Tony Burcher was reporting for duty at RAF Coningsby.

The No. 106 Squadron to which Tony arrived in the late spring of 1942 was rapidly gaining a reputation as one of the 'crack' units in No. 5 Group and the whole of Bomber Command. This was perhaps not surprising, given that the squadron had recently received a new officer commanding – Wing Commander Guy Gibson. Its flight commanders were no less impressive: Squadron Leader John 'Dim' Wooldridge, DFC, DFM, was a former sergeant pilot of considerable experience. He would go on to add a bar to his earlier DFC and command No. 105 Squadron; Squadron Leader Francis Robertson, DFC, a southern Rhodesian, was also an experienced operator and one of Gibson's inner circle.

Their OC, meanwhile, polarized opinions: to some, he was little short of a god; to others, a fanatic who would drive both men and machines beyond their physical endurance. Not for nothing was he quickly nicknamed 'the boy emperor' by the ground crews – an accolade that was not meant as a compliment.

The squadron had only recently exchanged its outdated Handley Page Hampdens for the rather disappointing twin-engined Avro Manchester. This brief flirtation did not last long, however, and soon after the crews began converting to the Man-

chester's rather more illustrious successor, the Avro Lancaster, and never looked back.

Tony was allowed some time to settle in before being listed on the Battle Order for his first operation, albeit a historic one. The squadron put up some fifteen Lancaster and Manchester aircraft to take part in an attack on Essen on the night of 1/2 June – one of the first of the Bomber Command C-in-C's showpiece thousand-bomber raids. Captain of Tony's Lancaster was an experienced senior NCO, Warrant Officer Peter Merralls, DFM (later DFC, DFM). Merralls had won the distinguished flying medal for a tour of operations with No. 49 Squadron, and would become somewhat of a celebrity, appearing in *Life* magazine in an article headlined 'Captain Pete bombs Cologne'.

On the night of 25/26 June, Tony was again selected for operations and another thousand-bomber trip, but this time to Bremen with a novice pilot with whom he would go on to complete his first tour and who would himself go on to become a distinguished Pathfinder: Sergeant James Cassels. 'Jock' Cassels had arrived at 106 at much the same time as Tony, and flown a handful of 'second dickey' trips in May, such that he was now considered ready to captain his own aircraft. The author of the squadron's Operations Record Book was in no doubt as to the success of the operation: 'For the Squadron, the raid cannot be classed as anything but outstanding.'

Towards the end of July, Tony was the mid-upper gunner in Jock's aircraft when they were chased by a nightfighter over Duisburg, but managed to escape. Less than a week later, and they were again intercepted, but this time with rather more conclusive results. The combat report tells its own dramatic story:

On the night of 29/30th July a Lancaster 'M' was attacked at 0052 while flying at 10,000 feet by a single-engined aircraft, at position 5140 N 0230 E. The enemy aircraft came in from the starboard quarter at the same height firing cannon from 500 yards. The Lancaster took evasive action losing height to 5,000 feet. The enemy aircraft was lost and our own aircraft did not return fire.

At 0117 hours at 10,000 feet 15 miles SE of Lille, Lancaster 'M' was attacked by an unidentified aircraft. The enemy aircraft came in from starboard beam, tracer passed

'Sergeant Burcher has completed a tour of operational duty during which he has displayed the greatest enthusiasm and keenness. He has taken part in attacks against German and Italian targets and mining sorties off France and in the Baltic. He also flew as rear-gunner in the daylight raids on Danzig and Le Creusot. In July 1942 when returning from Saarbrucken his aircraft was attacked by five enemy fighters. This Airman's excellent commentaries enabled his Captain to evade two of them and his well-directed fire drove off another two and assisted in the destruction of the fifth. Throughout his tour Sergeant Burcher has displayed cheerfulness, courage and determination worthy of the greatest praise'.

Right Citation for the award of the Distinguished Flying Medal, London Gazette 20 April 1943.

ahead of the aircraft, rear gunner and mid-upper gunner returned the fire. The enemy aircraft was then seen to pass from starboard to port a few feet below the Lancaster; the enemy aircraft was then lost.

Five minutes after leaving the target approximately 20 miles west of Saarbrucken at 0220 hours at 5,500 feet a single-engined enemy aircraft was sighted by the rear gunner of the Lancaster dead astern at approximately 400 yards. It passed from astern to port quarter and opened fire with cannon at about 200 yards. The rear gunner returned the fire and the fighter passed then from port to starboard; as he did so tracer was seen to enter the enemy aircraft's fuselage. The enemy aircraft then passed to the starboard beam to make another attack. The mid-upper gunner gave instructions to the pilot to turn to starboard into the attack; as the pilot did so the enemy aircraft closed in on the starboard beam to 150 yards and the mid-upper gunner opened fire and tracer was seen to enter the engine and fuselage.

The enemy aircraft then broke [sic] into flames and dived to the ground. It was seen to crash by the observer, mid-upper and rear gunners. The pilot also saw it burning on the ground.

The enemy aircraft was claimed as definitely destroyed. At 0225 hours near Soulay while flying at 7,500 feet the Lancaster was shadowed for ten minutes by two unidentified aircraft. One on the starboard beam that did not open fire and one astern that opened fire from 600 yards. The pilot then took evasive action and both aircraft were lost.

The crew returned safely.

Further ops followed, including trips to Mainz (12 August), Düsseldorf (15 August) and Kassel (27 August), when they were forced north of track by strong defences. Four trips in September were interrupted with the squadron's move from Coningsby to Syerston, and an operation on 1 October that proved very nearly their last. Ordered to attack Wismar, their aircraft was coned by searchlights and immediately hit by flak. Jock pushed the aircraft's nose down to escape, losing more than 10,000 feet before finally pulling out at 2,500 feet and jettisoning his bombs.

Perhaps the highlight of Tony's tour at 106 was a showpiece daylight attack that had the officer commanding, Guy Gibson, leading the squadron. Nearly 100 bombers flew to the target – the Schneider factory at Le Creusot – in formation at treetop level, only breaking formation for their bombing run. A contemporary of Burcher's, Pilot

Officer R. A. Wellington, described the operation as 'both successful and enjoyable'. The Cassel crew reported seeing direct hits on the factory.

By the end of November, Tony's first operational tour was coming to an end, and his abilities as an air gunner were recognized in three different ways: the award of the distinguished flying medal; a posting to Central Gunnery School (CGS) to complete a Gunnery Leader's course; and a commission. His joy, however, was tempered by some terrible news from home concerning the death of his brother Stephen, fighting the Japanese in Papua New Guinea.

Like all aircrew having completed his tour, Tony was entitled to six months' 'rest'. With the dangers facing his own native land, however, and the poignancy of his brother's death, there was a

Above John Fraser, proudly displaying the single-wing brevet of 'The flying arsehole'. *(Shere Fraser McCarthy)*

suggestion that he might be able to return home. A considerably higher authority decided this was not to be, and Tony found himself posted to 1654 Conversion Unit (CU) at Wigsley as an instructor. But his posting did not last. Within two months he was on his way to Scampton and a very special squadron.

As Tony Burcher was coming to the end of his first operational tour, 25 miles further north at Skellingthorpe, home to No. 50 Squadron, John Fraser was just starting out on his. As part of 5 Group, 50 Squadron was similar to No. 106 Squadron in that

No. 25 OTU (RAF Finningley) under the command of a fellow Canadian, Sergeant Norman Schofield. John was the air bomber.

Schofield, affectionately known as 'Pop' on account of his age (he was then 28), was almost immediately on the Battle Order, flying a 'second-dickey' trip to Genoa (unsuccessfully as it turned out) on the night of 13/14 November. Ten days later, John found himself on the Battle Order as part of the crew of Flying Officer E. N. Goldsmith. He wrote of the experience to his family on 23 November 1942:

it had recently replaced its Manchesters with Lancasters, and was also gaining a proud reputation for 'pressing on'. The example was being set by its officer commanding, Wing Commander William Russell, DFC (later Bar), a Canadian who had won his first DFC with the same squadron two years earlier. (Russell would later be killed in action with 138 Squadron in May 1944.) He exemplified the spirit of the squadron motto: 'Thus we keep faith.'

John reported to the squadron from No. 9 Conversion Flight (Waddington) on 9 November 1942. Unlike Tony, however, John arrived as part of a whole crew that had earlier met and trained at

Last night I did go on 'ops' – not with my own crew, but as a fill-in bomb aimer on another crew. Last night was a good success as far as our crew was concerned – we got the aiming point in the centre of the photograph of where the bombs burst. Quite lucky I am that on my first trip on the squadron I got such good results. I'm not shooting a line either – just plain honest to God facts.

The crew flew its first operation together on 6/7 December, a comparatively 'easy' gardening (that is, mine-laying) trip, followed by two ops to Turin. John wrote (somewhat poetically!) of the experience a little later:

For the last two nights I've been to Italy – as you most probably saw in the papers – we gave them hell both nights – I would not care to live in Turin now or what there is left of it. The Alps are beautiful at night – covered with snow – when I went to Italy 10-days ago the moon was just past full moon, but it did light up the mountains wonderfully.

In a short space of time, John was beginning to make his mark on the squadron, earning the nickname 'Fearless Fraser'. He was also fitting into squadron life, comforted by the occasional food parcel to remind him of home. On 10 December he wrote:

Thanks for the parcel. I was getting short of shirts and it arrived just in time for our next leave in approximately two weeks' time. You know where the nuts, cookies, cheese, peanut butter, gum, [and] chocolate bars went – right into my stomach – the parcel travelled well and everything was swell. I had about ½ tin of Nescafé left from a former parcel – sure makes a warm drink in the evening before crawling into bed. We'll make some soup one of these nights too and the pineapple juice – I haven't tasted anything like it for so long I could hardly believe it.

While John and the crew enjoyed a comparatively 'soft' introduction to operations, there was nothing easy about the target to be attacked on the night of 16/17 January – Berlin. A dangerous trip at any stage of the war, it nearly proved the crew's undoing. Heading home, some 65 miles to the north-west of the city, the Lancaster – which had already been damaged by flak – suddenly came under attack from a Junkers 88 nightfighter. Cannon and machine-gun fire smashed home, shattering the rear turret and severely injuring the rear gunner, Sergeant 'Johnnie' Bell. Only when the Junkers came into attack the second time did the mid-upper gunner (Sergeant Baker) manage to fire off a long burst at very short range, seeing his tracer enter the belly of the machine, which broke off trailing smoke from its port engine. Schofield, meanwhile, had put the Lancaster into a steep dive, losing more than 8,000 feet before levelling out and heading for home. The drama was far from over, and is brought into sharp relief by another of John's letters home:

We really bombed Berlin as they did London . . . 'Pop' deserves a medal for bringing us back. Our rear gunner is in hospital with a cannon shell through his right arm and another through his ankle. The kite was a mess of holes: a flak hole in the bomb doors that you could put your head and shoulders through, controls to the elevator shot away. Pop and I held the nose of the plane down with a haywire scheme with the trailing aerial wire for 600 miles, while the flight engineer joined the wires to the controls in the back. The navigator did a bang-up job, while the wireless operator gave Johnnie hot coffee and oxygen.

Below
An expression of condolence to the Fraser family from the Canadian Government.
(Shere Fraser McCarthy)

The compressed air tanks were punctured and Pop could not blow down the landing carriage but he jarred one wheel down and bounced the plane . . . we had no brakes, so we taxied along on an angle until we buried ourselves in a mud-hole. The trip looks better in my log book than it did then.

A week later, and the crew very nearly came to grief again. This time they were on their way back from Düsseldorf and 10 miles south of Utrecht when Sergeant F. C. Basham, in the mid-upper turret, spotted an aircraft some 800 yards away on a reciprocal course. Three minutes later, the replacement rear gunner (Sergeant Brian Jagger) identified a Bf110 coming in from the port quarter down, and called for the pilot to turn to port and dive, presenting him with a decent shot. Both gunners opened up, just as the nightfighter also started shooting. The rear turret was again hit and an electric circuit damaged, causing an inspection lamp to flick on unexpectedly, temporarily robbing the gunner of his night vision. The mid-upper gunner was also hit and wounded in the right arm. Despite this, as the Messerschmitt passed again to the rear, the gunners filled its belly with tracer, seeing it roll over, seemingly out of control and confident enough to claim it as probably destroyed.

The regular navigator, Canadian Pilot Officer Ken ('George') Earnshaw, wrote about this raid soon after, and how close they came to disaster:

We just saw him in time, but even at that he got in quite a burst at us. Our mid upper gunner was hit and our plane was riddled with bullet holes. We managed, however, to get home okay and the wounded gunner is doing fine too. It could have been a lot worse. Well, I guess as long as one is around to tell of these things they really aren't that bad, are they? Ha! Ha!

After the excitement of the previous fortnight, the crew settled into a routine of operations, at some considerable pace, flying no fewer than eight in February and nine in March, including three further trips to Berlin – happily without incident. Two attacks on Duisburg on consecutive nights at the beginning of April brought John's tour to a conclusion, by which time he had chalked up thirty-one operations (including one while still at OTU) and a further two ops noted in his logbook as 'DNCO' – duty not carried out.

John now had a choice: he was entitled to six months' 'rest' – perhaps at an OTU imparting his experience to others – or he could request to continue operations. Should he complete a further twenty trips (the criteria for a second tour), he could return home and be out of the war for good. There was also another influence: while at Finningley he had met Doris Wilkinson, a young secretary. As the months had gone by their affection had turned to love, and they were shortly to be married.

It proved to be a busy and eventful month: an interview for a commission; a wedding to his sweetheart; and a posting to a new squadron to commence his second tour.

In the weeks prior to John's arrival at Scampton, the squadron had been fully occupied with hour upon hour of cross-country and low-level training flights, both during the day and at night. Wing Commander Gibson, the man handpicked to lead this 'special' unit, had chosen his pilots with great care, and both Tony and John found themselves in the crew of Flight Lieutenant John Hopgood.

Hopgood was an Englishman raised in the village of Shere on the outskirts of Guildford, Surrey. Gentle yet determined, he had accumulated a commendable operational record with both 50 and 106 Squadrons – certainly enough to earn him two awards for gallantry. Gibson himself described Hopgood as 'probably the best pilot on the squadron'.

On 23 April, John wrote to Doris, briefly outlining the men in his new crew:

There is one Australian P/O DFM in the crew called Tony, one Scot P/O DFM called Jack, a sergeant wireless op called Minchie, a navigator P/O called Ossie, engineer sergeant called Charlie (a Canadian who came over here seven years ago and settled in Leeds, an attempt to colonize this country), the pilot called 'Hoppy' (F/L DFC and Bar), and me. I feel a bit strange after flying with Pop, but everything should work out OK.

What happened to the original navigator is not clear, for he was shortly after replaced by George Earnshaw, no doubt much to John's delight. Bomb aimer and navigator often worked closely together, and that was much easier when a bond of trust and friendship had already been established.

The intensity of training increased, John getting to grips with the Dann bombsight, a somewhat Heath Robinson affair that had been knocked up in the station workshops and that would enable the bomb aimer to drop his secret weapon at the correct distance from the target. At last, the day of the operation arrived and the targets were revealed. The reason behind the need for extremely accurate low-level flying over water at night had now become clear.

The crews were divided into three waves, and Hopgood was selected to fly with Gibson and seven other pilots in the second wave, whose target was the Möhne and Eder Dams. Take-off was an impressive affair, the first three aircraft of the group (Gibson, Hopgood and 'Mickey' Martin) thundering down the runway in vic formation and lifting off together at 2139 hours.

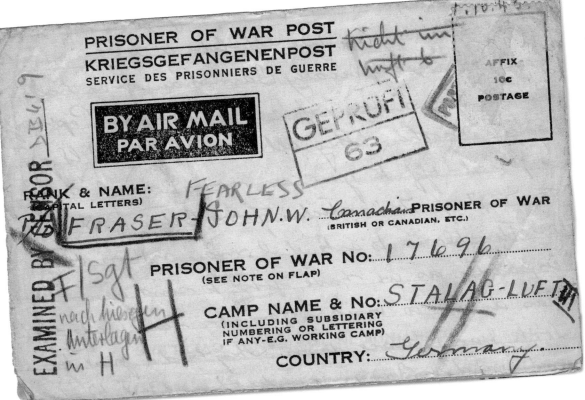

Left John's prisoner of war identity card. The date of capture is given as 17 May. *(Shere Fraser McCarthy)*

Left One of John's first letters home from Stalag Luft III. Note John's nickname: 'Fearless'. *(Shere Fraser McCarthy)*

In Hopgood's aircraft M-Mother, the crew busied themselves with their duties. Aircrew would often speak of sometimes being too busy to be scared, and perhaps this was one of those occasions. The enemy coast came and went quickly by, each of the aircraft being a little off track having underestimated the winds. The Lancasters eased themselves lower to the ground, but were soon after picked up by searchlights and on the receiving end of some light flak. Hopgood took avoiding action, taking the aircraft so low that he actually flew underneath some high-tension cables, frightening himself and his crew as a result.

It began to go wrong over Dulmen: flak, which they had so far seen but avoided, this time caught up with them and inflicted serious damage. Tony smelled the unmistakable aroma of cordite in the aircraft and noted that the port outer engine had been hit and was on fire. He had also been hit himself, sustaining slight injuries to his stomach and groin. Others had not been so lucky: John Minchin, the wireless operator, had been more seriously hurt and could not move his legs; the skipper was hit and bleeding from a head wound; and there was no response to his captain's calls from George Gregory in the front turret.

With one of his crew possibly dead, one seriously wounded, and one other with minor injuries, Hopgood would have had every justification in abandoning their mission. But he did not. In the best traditions of the RAF and the desire to 'press on regardless', Hopgood remained steadfast to his task.

M-Mother arrived at the Möhne, and the three aircraft in the first flight – Gibson, Hopgood and Martin – began orbiting the target. There were no balloons or searchlights to contend with, but every crew was mindful of the flak guns positioned on the dam and in the immediate vicinity. Gibson flew a dummy run before committing to the attack, reminding Hopgood to be ready to assume command should something happen. Then he went in, and had the great satisfaction of seeing his bomb skip across the water toward the dam, followed by a terrific explosion and a great spurt of water leaping into the air. But the dam held. Hopgood had an anxious wait before his attack. The water needed to settle and the spray to clear. Indeed M-Mother held off for a further five minutes before Gibson finally gave his deputy the order to attack, reassuring Hopgood that it was 'a piece of cake'. It was to prove anything but.

Gibson had the advantage of catching the German flak batteries off guard. By the time Hopgood came in to attack, however, they were more than ready for him, and an almost predictable tragedy unfolded. Tony and John were at exact opposite ends of their aircraft. Tony was at the rear and could see nothing, save for the vicious streaks of tracer passing close by his turret; he prepared to shoot at the flak gunners once they were over the dam. John, on the other hand, had arguably the best seat in the house, but, as he held the bombsight in front of him, and waited for the release point, the aircraft was hit and almost immediately burst into flames. The bomb was seen to release but a fraction too late, and instead of hitting the dam it skipped over the wall and exploded in a power station a little way beyond.

A red Very light was fired from the aircraft, in accordance with instructions, to indicate that the bomb had been dropped, but by now one wing was almost enveloped in flames and the aircraft appeared all but doomed. Hopgood desperately tried to gain height to give his crew a chance to bale out,

Rheinberg War Cemetery and the resting place of F/Lt John Hopgood and four of his crew, Sgt Charles Brennan, F/O Kenneth Earnshaw, Sgt John Minchin, P/O George Gregory. *(Fighting High)*

and with only two engines still functioning managed to struggle up to around 500 feet before the aircraft exploded and plunged burning to the ground.

In the thirty or so seconds from the time that the aircraft cleared the dam to the moment it exploded, the activity within the aircraft had been frantic. Both pilot and flight engineer had tried desperately and against overwhelming odds to extinguish the flames, before Hopgood gave in to the inevitable and shouted for the crew to bale out.

John, in the nose, needed no second bidding and opened the escape hatch to see the tops of the trees

Right The headstone of 21-year-old F/Lt John Vere Hopgood, DFC, and Bar at the Rheinberg War Cemetery, grave reference 17–E, 2-6. (collective grave). *(Fighting High)*

uncomfortably close. Ignoring what he had been taught, he clipped on his parachute and pulled his ripcord inside the cockpit, letting the parachute billow out in front of him and pull him out after it. At the rear, Tony was faced with a similar dilemma. With the loss of hydraulics, and therefore power, he had been obliged to crank his turret round by hand in double quick time to get back into the fuselage and retrieve his parachute. With his usual escape route blocked, he too was obliged to ignore the manual and jump from the rear door. But as he was planning to leave the aircraft, he was suddenly halted by the sight of the badly injured John Minchin edging his way down the fuselage towards him. Tony took the only decision he could, and pushed Minchin out of the aircraft, pulling his D-ring as he went and hoping for the best. He then prepared to jump himself, also pulling his ripcord inside the aircraft and gathering the silk in his arms at the very moment that the aircraft exploded. Tony was blasted out through the entrance and suddenly and painfully understood why using the crew entrance door was discouraged as his back struck the Lancaster's tail fin.

As he tumbled out of the front hatch, John distinctly remembered seeing the tail wheel whizzing past his ear and then within less than two or three seconds hitting the ground. What happened next is difficult to determine with 100 per cent certainty, and stories have undoubtedly become confused over time. According to official records, including his German prisoner of war *Personalkarte*, John was captured on the same day that he was shot down. In the section marked *Gefangennahme* – literally 'taken prisoner' – it reads 'Soest. 17.5.43'. This appears to be confirmed in another record held by the Canadian archive reporting: 'INFORMATION RECEIVED FROM GENEVA 24 JUNE STATES BERLIN CABLES FOLLOWING CAPTURED R73769 SERGEANT ALLAN K T 17/4 R106546 FLIGHT SERGEANT FRASER J W 17/5.' There is also no mention of John evading capture in his 'Questionnaire for returned evaders, escapers and prisoner of war'.

Documents therefore point to John being captured on 17 May. John's family, however, have a different and very definite memory of what happened. According to them John managed to make his escape from the immediate area and evaded for ten days, living off the land, before finally being captured, exhausted, near the Dutch border. Whether caught immediately or some time after, John finished his war in a POW camp, first in Stalag Luft VI and later (once his commission had been confirmed) at the officers' camp at Stalag Luft III, the scene of the Great Escape.

What happened to Tony is equally obscure. The injuries to his back sustained upon hitting the tail fin left him in no position to make good his escape. Landing in a recently ploughed field undoubtedly helped cushion his landing, but his back was seriously damaged and possibly even broken. He also had a cracked a kneecap. Despite being in considerable pain, Tony managed to crawl towards a culvert, where he hid for almost three days before finally surrendering to a young Hitler Youth. His memory of those days, and what happened immediately afterwards, were confused by delirium brought on by his injuries and lack of food and water, save for a few Horlicks tablets his mother had sent him and that he had had the foresight to take with him that night. In letters and interviews many years after the war, Tony claims to have been interrogated by a German with an Australian accent, and doggedly revealed only his name, rank and number. He credits the treatment given to him by the German doctor who tended to his injuries as being the reason he was still able to walk. That may or may not have been true, but what we do know for certain, and the records confirm it, is that Tony ended his war as a prisoner in Stalag Luft III.

John and Tony met in camp, but perhaps surprisingly never reunited after the war. John took his young wife with him back to Canada, where they had two sons and a daughter: the boys were named John and Guy, and the daughter, Shere, after the village in which Hoppy Hopgood had lived. It was their tribute to the man that John said saved his life. John senior achieved his ambition to fly, and became president of the Nanaimo Flying Club. Sadly he did not long survive the war: in June 1962, while on an aerial survey flight of log booms near Saltery Bay, his aircraft crashed and he was killed.

Tony's fortunes were rather more mixed. Although he determined to remain in the Air Force after the war, he never settled. He married Joan, an English WAAF he had met at Coningsby, in June 1945, and returned to Australia, but she struggled with being so far from home and her family. In early 1950 he applied for and was granted a posting to serve in the UK, but a succession of commanding officers expressed dismay at his attitude and behaviour, the more generous describing him as 'unsatisfactory'. It is interesting to note that in many of his records his peers cite his exceptional war record in mitigation, but such sympathy could not last. His honesty and sense of propriety were called into question more than once, and tales of financial irregularities were never far away. It was perhaps a relief when he resigned his commission, and left the Service in February 1952.

Sadly, Tony's peers appear to have been good judges of character, for some years later, in 1963, the former Dam Buster was gaoled for two years for fraud. Even after this incident and his release, his name was frequently attached to a succession of dubious business ventures. Tony had always lived life on the edge, but was inclined too often to step beyond it. He died in Tasmania in 1995, his reputation sadly tarnished by his post-war peccadilloes.

It is hard for us to envisage what it must have been like for these men, serving their country, so far from home. It is difficult also to imagine the extremes of excitement and terror that must have accompanied them throughout their respective operational tours. Given their magnificent war record, it seems a pity that both men were cheated out of the happy ending they so richly deserved. What should always be remembered, however, is the courage, and the bravery of their skipper, Hoppy Hopgood. ●

CHAPTER FOUR

'I THINK SO, STAND BY'

ROBERT URQUHART, DFC

BY ROBERT OWEN

ACCURATE NAVIGATION WAS A VITAL ELEMENT OF OPERATION CHASTISE. FLYING THAT NIGHT IN ED937, AJ-Z, WITH THE 'B' FLIGHT COMMANDER, SQUADRON LEADER HENRY MAUDSLAY, WAS THE FLIGHT'S NAVIGATION OFFICER, FLYING OFFICER ROBERT URQUHART, WHO HAILED FROM MOOSE JAW, SASKATCHEWAN, WHERE, BY COINCIDENCE, HIS PILOT HAD COMPLETED HIS ADVANCED FLYING TRAINING. ALMOST ONE-THIRD OF THE NAVIGATORS INVOLVED WERE MEMBERS OF THE ROYAL CANADIAN AIR FORCE, NO MEAN ACHIEVEMENT WHEN NAVIGATION OVER THE INTENSE LAND-SCAPE OF WESTERN EUROPE WAS A FAR CRY FROM THE WIDE OPEN PRAIRIE OF THEIR NATIVE LAND.

BORN ON 2 AUGUST 1919, Urquhart was the eldest of two sons of Canadian Pacific Railways' accountant Alexander James Urquhart and his wife Susie Grace, who also had two daughters. After attending the King George Public School, Robert transferred to the Moose Jaw Collegiate Institute at the age of 14 for a year before completion of a four-year drafting course at Moose Jaw Technical High School. He was a diligent student, and also participated in a range of sports including baseball, rugby, hockey and track events.

In 1937 his father secured him his first job as a crew call boy for Canadian Pacific Railways. Within six months he had found himself a more creative outlet, an engraving apprenticeship with Eiler's Jewellery Store, Moose Jaw. Despite showing promise, in 1939 he switched jobs again, moving to Vancouver, as a buyer and stock controller for the Aristocratic Hamburger Company.

Following the outbreak of war, in common with many Canadians of eligible age, Robert was drawn to military service. In October 1940, while waiting for a decision on his written application to the RCAF, he completed a month's training as a private and acting lance corporal in the 2nd Battalion

Seaforth Highlanders of Canada. His RCAF application was finally accepted, and on 8 January 1941, at the Vancouver recruiting centre, he passed a medical, fit for training as a pilot or observer, and applied for a commission. The following day he reported as an AC2 at No. 2 Manning Depot, Brandon. On 11 April he was posted as a member of 23 Course at No. 2 Initial Training School, housed in Regina College and Regina Normal School, Regina, Saskatchewan, for evaluation as a member of aircrew. He came 55th out of 232, rated as above average, steady, alert and with quick reactions. Promoted to LAC and having acquired the sobriquet 'Turk', on 28 May 1941 he arrived for pilot training on 29 Course at No. 2 Elementary Flying Training School, formerly Thunder Bay Air Training School, at Fort William, Ontario.

He made his first flight, lasting forty-five minutes, on 1 June, but any initial euphoria, and the allocation of flying pay, was short-lived. It soon became clear that he lacked the coordination required by a competent pilot. After he had completed 10 hours 05 minutes' flying, his instructor decreed that he should be scrubbed as a pilot. While his ground work was 'average' and behaviour 'satisfactory', his ability to control the Tiger Moth was lacking. On take-off he would move the stick to one side and then hard back, instigating a swing and making no attempt to correct. His flying was extremely poor and inaccurate, completely lacking air sense or any idea of manœuvre. Landing, he ignored a conventional approach, simply flying to within a few feet of the ground before pulling the stick hard back, stalling the aircraft on to the ground. 'He shows no promise of getting the hang of flying.' There was no question of sending him solo.

He was despatched to Trenton on 15 June 1941 'for disposal'. Here the Composite School was responsible for assessing and reallocating scrubbed RCAF, RAF, RAAF and RNZAF pilots under training in Canada. A fortnight later he was recategorized as an air observer, reporting to No. 6 Air Observers' School at Prince Albert on 2 August. He was to spend two months on No. 30 Course, learning the craft of navigation in the unit's draughty Ansons. He had finally found his niche, being assessed as 'above average in nearly all subjects. A very good man, responsible and cool

Left Robert Urquhart prior to enlistment. He was noted for his smart and dapper appearance. *(National Archives of Canada)*

headed . . . suitable as an instructor.'

Training continued at No. 5 Bombing and Gunnery School, Dafoe, where, in obsolescent Fairey Battles (and surviving a forced landing because of an oil leak), he practised the duties of both bomb aimer and gunner. Scoring 'above average' for the former and 'average' as the latter – 'he should make a good air observer' – he was awarded his air observer's brevet on 6 December, being promoted to temporary sergeant. Two days later saw the start of the final stage of his training, astro navigation, on No. 30 Course at No. 1 Air Navigation School, Rivers, Manitoba. However, although he had a better grasp of astro than his results would suggest, he was inclined to make careless errors at times. His anticipated instructor's posting would not be forthcoming.

His commission was granted on 4 January 1942, and he was sent to Y Depot at Halifax prior to posting overseas. After a period of holding and ten days' embarkation leave, he returned to the depot to board the troop ship that was to bring him to the UK. Arriving at No. 3 Personnel Reception Centre at Bournemouth on 24 March, he was posted a month later to No. 2 (Observer) Advanced Flying Unit, Millom, Cumbria (now HMP Haverigg). Reacquainted with the Anson, he would familiarize himself with the different scale and visual appearance of the European landscape, the variable weather and the difficulties of navigation over a blacked-out countryside.

His future allocation to Bomber Command was now confirmed, with a posting to No. 14 Operational Training Unit, Cottesmore, on 19 May 1942. With a little more experience he might have been among the unit's pupils participating in the three 'Millennium' attacks against Cologne, Bremen and Essen, but it was not to be. However, instead of the more usual 'nickel' run, dropping leaflets over occupied territory, Robert's first operation was to be on the night of 31 July/1 August, against Düsseldorf, in a Hampden flown by Pilot Officer P. D. McGee. By the time the crew arrived the target was alight, aiding navigation, and their four

500-pounders were released from 11,000 feet over the centre of the town. Engine problems and shortage of fuel resulted in the aircraft landing at Wattisham on the return. Also concurrently passing through the OTU were other trainees who would participate with distinction on Chastise: Sergeant Les Knight and Pilot Officer Joe McCarthy. As the course came to an end and they prepared for posting to an operational squadron, Robert was reassured to find his navigational skills assessed as 'above average'.

Ten days later, on 24 August, he arrived at RAF Swinderby, home to No. 50 Squadron, to join the crew of 'A' Flight Commander, Squadron Leader Philip Moore. The squadron operated Lancasters, and, under the recently introduced Pilot, Navigator, Bomb Aimer (PNB) scheme, Robert would relinquish his bomb-aiming role to concentrate on navigation. Within four days of his arrival his crew was one of 12 from the squadron detailed to join a 159-aircraft force bound for Nuremberg. At this period No. 50 Squadron was perfecting its accuracy by making medium-level attacks. The crew had to release the bombs after running into the target at only 9,000 feet, after pinpointing a river and canal in bright moonlight, but no results were seen, for almost immediately the aircraft was caught in searchlights, providing a few tense moments until they were shaken off.

Karlsruhe was the target on the night of 2/3 September. There was only moderate opposition that night, and the target was well illuminated by marker flares, with the dock basins clearly identified, so the crew added its bombs to the conflagration below from 8,000 feet. The following night the Atlas shipyards at Bremen were the target. From 9,500 feet the river and docks were easily picked out, which facilitated an accurate attack. This precision was not to be repeated on 8/9 September, when, unsure of their position, the Pathfinders scattered flares over a wide area, resulting in the bulk of loads falling on Russelsheim instead of the intended target of Frankfurt. Thinking that they recognized the target by the shape of the river, Robert and his crew released their bombs from 10,000 feet, only to realize their error after bombing, as they passed over Frankfurt before turning for home. Two nights later the searchlights and flak were very active over Düsseldorf as they released a 4,000-pounder and 30-lb incendiaries from 10,500 feet, seeing buildings disintegrating in the bomb bursts.

On 12 September Robert was posted 'non-effective/sick' and was hospitalized at RAF Halton with a minor infection. He would return to the squadron on the 23rd, and a week later was promoted to Flying Officer.

Poor weather made navigation difficult for an attack on Aachen on 5/6 October, and the aircraft 'spent a lot of time wandering around France, avoiding defended areas', arriving late on target, where bombs were released on dead reckoning but no results were seen. Bad weather the following night resulted in difficulty finding Osnabrück. After circling a couple of times, guided by PFF flares, the bomb aimer spotted a built-up area, assumed to be the target, and bombs were released after a timed run from a nearby lake. A week later Robert's skills were put to the test when operating against Kiel.

The Gee (electronic navigation aid) set went u/s, and navigation was dependent upon dead reckoning and loop bearings. Once again a timed run from a nearby lake saved the day, and Robert was complemented in the squadron's Operations Record Book: 'This trip was notable for outstanding navigation.'

Participation in the unopposed daylight formation attack on Le Creusot of 17 October presented no navigational difficulties. But the weather proved trying again on 22/23 October; the crew pinpointed Northampton, but then cloud hid the ground until Robert's accurate navigation brought them over the Alps to Genoa, where the harbour outline was seen. Two days later another trans-Alpine trip brought them to a cloud-covered Milan, where they descended to 4,000 feet to bomb the already burning town. Further trips to Genoa were made on the nights of 6 and 7 November. On the second of these, immediately after bombing and leaving the target with bomb doors still open, the Lancaster shuddered as it was hit by flak. As they climbed to 16,000 feet, the port inner engine burst into flame. The fire was extinguished and the propeller feathered, but the port outer engine now also indicated rising temperature, which required constant monitoring for the return journey. Maintaining safety height to clear the Alps, they returned without further incident. A week later the crew were once more over Genoa, again sustaining minor flak damage, and they landed at Waddington on return.

At this point Squadron Leader Moore completed his tour, and Robert found himself as an experienced, but 'spare bod', seeking a new crew. On 17/18 December he found himself flying with Squadron Leader Birch and crew when the squadron despatched five aircraft as part of a small twenty-seven-aircraft attack against the marshalling yards at Soltau. Although it was a bright moonlit

who was commencing his second tour after a period as instructor at No. 1654 CU. Their first trip to Essen on 21/22 January was inauspicious. Thick haze made identification of ground detail impossible, and no PFF flares were seen. After loitering for thirty minutes, the crew bombed what they believed to be a genuine fire in the Ruhr area, but not before significant flak had damaged the port wing and tailplane. The same aircraft suffered minor damage to both wings six nights later over Düsseldorf, while the crew searched for a break in the cloud that enabled them to bomb the final green marker. Accurate flashless flak was also experienced over Cologne on 2/3 February, but their fortunes improved two nights later when they

night, three of the squadron's aircraft had great difficulty in locating the target. However, Robert, aided by other crew members, had no problems in identifying the river Weser and then following the Nienburg–Soltau road to the target just south-east of the town. Despite lively light flak, they bombed from only 1,500 feet. A large building alongside the yards was seen to catch fire, with a substantial blue explosion being seen five minutes later. There was no sign of any other strikes. On the return they were attacked and damaged by fighters. During the action Robert sustained a minor injury, but Peter Birch brought the Lancaster safely back to base. Two of the squadron's aircraft were not so fortunate and failed to return.

In the new year Robert teamed up with a new captain, Flight Lieutenant Henry Maudslay, DFC,

went to Turin. Operations continued until the middle of the month, with attacks on Wilhelmshaven, Lorient and Milan. March saw a resumption of German targets: Hamburg on 3/4, Munich on 9/10, and Essen on 12/13, before attention was turned again to the U-boat offensive with an attack on Saint-Nazaire on 22/23 March.

The crew were now well into their tour and becoming key members of the squadron. However, in the third week of March, as with selected crews from other No. 5 Group units, they were abruptly posted to Scampton for the formation of a new squadron under the command of Wing Commander Gibson, formerly Officer Commanding No. 106 Squadron. The move was accompanied with a promotion for Maudslay, who became Squadron Leader and appointed 'B' Flight Commander of the new unit. In recognition of his expertise and exemplary record, Robert was appointed the flight's navigation officer.

No. 617 Squadron, as it was to become, soon began training for its as yet unspecified task. Robert reported to the squadron navigation officer, Flight Lieutenant Jack Leggo, and as flight navigation officer was responsible for overseeing ten navigators, reviewing their logs and addressing any difficulties. A number of set routes were established for the crews to follow, facilitating the work of the Observer Corps and hopefully reducing complaints about low flying. Henry Maudslay and his crew carried out their first daylight cross-country on 31

assist him the navigator had Gee – assuming that it was working and not jammed – and also the new Air Position Indicator, an analogue computer taking inputs of speed and course to calculate the aircraft's present position, displaying it as latitude and longitude on an odometer-style read-out. Although this was in short supply, the squadron was given priority. The device was not perfect and required occasional manual resetting, the navigator using reports of observed landmarks and his own expertise to update the position. It was realized that it would be imprudent to rely too heavily on these aids, so training was carried out using dead reckoning and pinpointing with drift sighting, using flame floats over the sea.

March in a borrowed No. 9 Squadron Lancaster with a further exercise on 3 April.

Owing to the navigator's restricted view, visual navigation would be performed by the bomb aimer, using large-scale roller maps produced in conjunction with the navigators. These maps would be carefully studied before flight and key pinpoints marked: water features, or bridges over rivers, would be most prominent at night. Navigators calculated the timing between each landmark and notified the bomb aimer of the next point's ETA, providing the pilot with course adjustments, based upon drift and speed. The navigator would be fully occupied performing these calculations, checking the aircraft's track and position. Drift was calculated using forecast winds, checked by drift sightings taken by the gunners and updated at turning points. To

Robert was also the first squadron navigator to experience the spotlight altimeter. The device had been resurrected by RAE technicians and on 4 April Maudslay flew a standard Lancaster to Farnborough, returning to Scampton four days later with the lights installed to demonstrate the equipment's accuracy.

The crew then began training in earnest. A 4 1/2-hour cross-country on 11 April was followed by a 2 1/2-hour daylight run on the 13th, followed by a 5-hour night flight. Strangely, after a 4 1/2-hour flight to the north of Scotland on 15 April, the crew did not fly during the period of the full moon, possibly to permit less experienced crews an opportunity to practise. By 16 April intensive practice was paying dividends, and most pinpoints were now being found exactly on ETA. Flying experience was

Reichswald Forest War Cemetery. Below (inset): The original cross bearing Robert Urquhart's name along with that of two of his colleagues, Flying Officer Tytherleigh and Pilot Officer Fuller, and a modern photograph showing their final resting place. *(National Archives of Canada and Fighting High)*

FLYING OFFICER
W.J. TYTHERLEIGH, DFC
AIR GUNNER
ROYAL AIR FORCE
17TH MAY 1943 AGE 21

120851   F.O. W. J. TYTHERLEIGH (DFC)
J.9763   F.O. R. A. URQUHART (DFC) RCAF
143760   P.O. M. J. D. FULLER
R.A.F.   17-5-43

supplemented by ground training. Navigators and bomb aimers attended the screening of a film emphasizing the importance of teamwork for low-level navigation, and a training room was established to refine use of the Gee set.

By the beginning of May training was rationalized. In addition to using the synthetic two-stage amber, crews were now undertaking short cross-countries at dusk to simulate moonlight flying. From 5 May training exercises were instigated over Eyebrook Reservoir, near Uppingham, sometimes also taking in Abberton Reservoir near Colchester, to practise operational tactics. On 8 May the crew first flew a Type 464 Lancaster, modified to carry Upkeep. The aircraft was taken up to test the prototype VHF radio installation that would enable Wing Commander Gibson to direct the crews while over the target.

With the deadline for the operation approaching, and with the crews still ignorant of the nature of their target, the squadron now began to practise dropping inert Upkeeps. Maudslay's opportunity came on 12 May when he flew down to Reculver. Because it was daylight, the spotlight altimeter could not be used, and the aircraft was too low on release. The rising plume of spray from the weapon's initial impact with the water struck the aircraft, tearing off a panel and distorting others. The aircraft was damaged, but still flyable, and Maudslay nursed it back to Scampton, where it was deemed too badly damaged to participate in the operation. The following day the crew reverted to a standard aircraft, for a bombing and tactics exercise. A replacement Type 464 aircraft was delivered on 14 May. After an air test and bombing detail, the crew flew it that night on what transpired to be the final exercise before Operation Chastise.

The morning of 16 May would have been one of intense activity as Robert was briefed on the planned route for the operation, prepared his flight plan, and checked those of others in his flight. By 1700 briefing was over and crews were heading for their respective Messes for the pre-flight meal. Then there was an opportunity for freshening up, writing a quick letter or generally getting organized, before it was time for crews to don flying clothing and wait for the buses to take them out to the aircraft. The Maudslay crew was detailed with Flight Lieutenant Astell and Pilot Officer Knight as the third section of the main formation heading for the Möhne Dam.

The three aircraft took off without incident at 2159, forming into a loose vic with Maudslay in the lead (although each navigator kept his own plot), and headed south-east to Southwold. Crossing the North Sea, they entered Holland over the Scheldt Estuary. All appears to have gone according to plan until reaching a T-shaped canal junction at Beek, east of Eindhoven, when Flight Lieutenant Astell fell behind in the turn. East of the next pinpoint at Rees, on the Rhine, the aircraft ran into light flak, further fragmenting the formation and from then on each proceeded independently, but only Maudslay and Knight would reach the Möhne.

Entering a holding pattern to the south and east of the target, out of range of the defences, the crew listened over the VHF to the progress of the attack, no doubt joining in the brief elation as the dam collapsed. But there was work to do. Robert gave his captain the prepared course for the Eder Dam, and the aircraft turned south-east. As ETA approached, Pilot Officer Michael Fuller, the bomb aimer, peered anxiously for sign of the target. The rolling terrain surrounding the Möhne Dam had transformed into steeper, twisting valleys that were now beginning to fill with mist, making identification of the reservoir difficult. With tension mounting, the crew would have seen the red Very light fired by Wing Commander Gibson, who had located the target. Along with Young, who was acting as Deputy Leader, Flight Lieutenant Shannon and Pilot Officer Knight, Maudslay's crew homed in on the Eder Dam to familiarize themselves with its topography. The briefing model had not been completed in time, and the crew had seen only photographs and maps, but already appreciated the difficulty of the task ahead. There was no flak, but protruding spurs prevented a straight and level approach to the target. Attacking aircraft would have to approach from behind the promontory (upon which was perched the village of Waldeck with its distinctive castle), diving steeply for a spit projecting into the lake and turning sharply to port before levelling out to attain the release parameters of 60 feet and 230 mph within half a mile, before reaching the release point 425

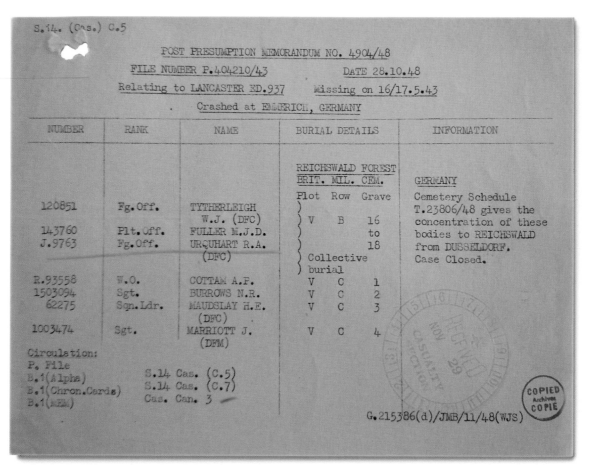

S.14. (Cas.) C.5

POST PRESUMPTION MEMORANDUM NO. 4904/48

FILE NUMBER P.404210/43   DATE 28.10.48

Relating to LANCASTER ED.937   Missing on 16/17.5.43

. Crashed at EMMERICH, GERMANY

NUMBER	RANK	NAME	BURIAL DETAILS			INFORMATION
			REICHSWALD FOREST BRIT. MIL. CEM.			GERMANY
			Plot	Row	Grave	Cemetery Schedule
120851	Fg.Off.	TYTHERLEIGH W.J. (DFC)	) V	B	16	T.23806/48 gives the concentration of these
143760	Plt.Off.	FULLER M.J.D.	)		to	bodies to REICHSWALD
J.9763	Fg.Off.	URQUHART R.A. (DFC)	)		18	from DUSSELDORF.
			) Collective			Case Closed.
			) burial			
R.93558	W.O.	COTTAM A.P.	V	C	1	
1503094	Sgt.	BURROWS N.R.	V	C	2	
62275	Sqn.Ldr.	MAUDSLAY H.E. (DFC)	V	C	3	
1003474	Sgt.	MARRIOTT J. (DFM)	V	C	4	

Circulation:
P. File
B.1(Alpha)   S.14 Cas. (C.5)
B.1(Chron.Cards)   S.14 Cas. (C.7)
B.1(MEM.)   Cas. Can. 3

G.215386(d)/JMB/11/48(WJS)

Left Details of the resting place of the crew of Lancaster ED937 as contained in Robert Urquhart's papers. *(National Archives of Canada)*

C O P Y   A.471471/42/S7B1

R.C.A.F. Overseas Headquarters
Lincoln's Inn Fields.   F/O R.A. Urquhart, (J9763) Nav.

In accordance with a recommendation from the A.O.C.-in-C.,
Bomber Command it has been decided to make a note in the following
terms on the records of personnel who took part in the raid on the
dams and failed to return:-

"On the night of the 16th/17th May 1943 this officer/
airman took part in the extremely hazardous and highly
successful raid on the Moehne, Eder, Sorpe and Schwelm
dams, from which operation he failed to return."

Extract from:
S.7.B.1
d/29.6.43.

Left Details of the recommended insertion into Robert Urquhart's files concerning involvement in Operation Chastise. *(National Archives of Canada)*

From left to right, W/O Alden Cottam, Sgt Norman Burrows, S/Ldr Henry Maudslay, Sgt John Marriott, at the Reichswald Forest War Cemetery. *(Fighting High)*

yards from the dam. At release, full power would be required, to enable the aircraft to execute a climbing turn to starboard to avoid a steep hillside rising 300 feet less than a mile ahead. There were only three Upkeeps, but, given the difficulties of approach, would these be sufficient?

Unsurprisingly, given the circumstances of this attack, official records and personal recollections conflict. There is no dispute as to the fact that both Maudslay and Shannon made a number of abortive attempts, both finding it exceedingly difficult to achieve the release criteria. As time passed Gibson's frustration began to manifest itself, and his radio communication acquired an impatient edge. It appears that Shannon may have finally made a successful attack, his Upkeep detonating to the right

by the force of the explosion, before being lost to sight against the black hillside. Unsure of what had happened, Gibson called several times over the VHF, asking Maudslay if he was all right. Eventually a faint reply was received: 'I think so, stand by.' The aircraft was still flying, although its condition and that of its crew must remain speculation. At Grantham a message was received 'Goner 28B' – 'mine released, overshot, no apparent breach' – although frustratingly the time of its receipt is corrupt.

As the Lancaster had crossed the dam, its crew, especially Robert, standing in the cockpit behind Sergeant John Marriott, the flight engineer, would have braced themselves for the steep climbing turn. This may have indirectly prepared them for the jolt

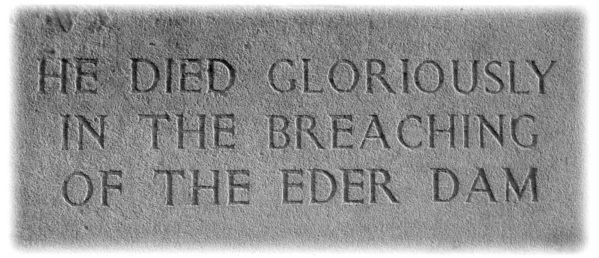

of the dam's centre – not surprising considering the line of attack. At about 0145 Maudslay was called in again. There is a record that something was seen hanging beneath the aircraft, which suggests that it may have been hit and damaged on the way out. Whether or not this had any influence on the events that followed is debatable. The Lancaster levelled out over the lake, having probably gained speed in the dive. There can have been little time for Urquhart to assess the spots and for Maudslay to respond to any instructions before Pilot Officer Fuller released their Upkeep. Whether it struck the water and bounced, or fell directly on to the target, cannot be ascertained, but those watching saw a gigantic flash on the parapet marginally behind and beneath the Lancaster, which was seen banking steeply away, its exit manœuvre possibly exaggerated

as the blast from Upkeep struck the aircraft, but nevertheless this unexpected event can only have tested Maudslay's airmanship to the limit, as he struggled to maintain control of the aircraft. After assessing their condition, the crew appear to have continued to fly their briefed route home – almost the reciprocal of their outward route as far as the Rhine, although their timings to reach this point suggest either a slower airspeed, or that they gave a wider berth to the defences; it is also possible that damage may have made it difficult to maintain course. No more is known of the aircraft's return flight until shortly before 0230, when flak gunners defending the port of Emmerich heard the sound of a large aircraft approaching low from the east. For whatever reason the aircraft was marginally off track and heading towards the town. As it came within range, 20mm light flak around the port area opened fire at minimum elevation, shells scything the tops off tall poplars as the gunners brought their sights to bear. The Lancaster turned to starboard to avoid their fire, but it was too late. There was a flash, and the aircraft caught fire, disappearing to the north, followed by the sound of an explosion as it fell to earth adjacent to a brickworks near to the small settlement of Netterden.

The following morning German officials inspected the wreckage, finding the remains of its seven crew, all of whom must have died instantly. All were recovered and taken to the Nord Friedhof in Düsseldorf, where they were laid to rest on 19 May, although such was their condition that only Sergeant Marriott and Sergeant Cottam could be positively identified. There they would remain, in the company of many other comrades from Bomber Command whose lives had ended prematurely in the skies over the Ruhr, until 1948, when representatives of the Imperial War Graves Commission began the sad task of exhumation prior to concentration and reinterment in the newly created War Cemetery at Reichswald, south-west of Kleve.

There was one final act. At the end of his service with No. 50 Squadron, on 20 March 1943, Wing Commander William Russell had signed a recommendation for a non-immediate award of the Distinguished Flying Cross for Flying Officer Urquhart, who had completed twenty-eight operations. The recommendation had been approved by Air Vice Marshal Cochrane on 4 May, but had then been lost in official channels. It surfaced in 1945 and, since it had been submitted prior to the recommended officer's death, it was approved and promulgated in the *London Gazette* on 29 July 1945. Writing to Robert's parents the following day, Colin Gibson, Canadian Minister for National Defence and Air, explained the delay rather confusingly: 'There were times when recollections of the most important incidents were deferred by the exigencies of the conflict.' The administrative process would continue to grind slowly, and it would be another four years before they received the actual award. There would be no formal investiture, nor official presentation. The medal was unceremoniously despatched by registered mail on 7 November 1949. ●

Below
Representation of a letter from the offices of the Minister of National Defence for Air to Mr and Mrs A.J. Urquhart.

July 30, 1945

Dear Mr and Mrs Urquhart

I regret indeed that such a long period of time has elapsed before evidence of the gallantry of your son, Flying Officer Robert Alexander Urquhart DFC, was announced, but I am sure that you and the members of your family will wish to know the circumstances surrounding the honour and distinction which have come to him through the award of the Distinguished Flying Cross.

The citation on which this award for great gallantry in the performance of his duty while serving with the Royal Canadian Air Force was made reads as follows:

'Since joining the squadron Flying Officer Urquhart has flown on many operations. At all times his navigation has been of the highest order and the successes achieved are due in no small measure to his skill. This officer took part in the daylight raids on Le Creusot and Milan and at other times on many heavily defended German targets. On one occasion during a low level raid on a target in North West Germany he was wounded by anti-aircraft fire but continued to navigate with accuracy. By his skill and determination Flying Officer Urquhart has set a high standard among his fellow navigators.'

When one is removed from the actual fighting areas one wonders why such matters should be delayed. There are some, however, who see the answer to the question as we remember the circumstances in which one found oneself during the battle, when for example there were times when recollection of the most important incidents were deferred by the exigencies of the conflict.

The personnel of the Force join with you in the pride that your gallant son's conduct in action has thus been recognized.

CHAPTER FIVE

'UPON THE ALTAR THE DEAREST AND THE BEST'

MELVIN YOUNG, DFC AND BAR

BY ARTHUR THORNING

MELVIN YOUNG'S LIFE LEADING UP TO OPERATION CHASTISE WAS NOTABLE. OF ANGLO-AMERICAN PARENTAGE, HE WAS EDUCATED AT SEVERAL SCHOOLS ON BOTH SIDES OF THE ATLANTIC, BEFORE ATTENDING TRINITY COLLEGE, OXFORD, WHERE HE ACHIEVED A GOOD DEGREE IN LAW AND ROWED IN THE BOAT RACE AGAINST CAMBRIDGE. HE LEARNED TO FLY WITH THE OXFORD UNIVERSITY AIR SQUADRON AND, FOLLOWING THE OUTBREAK OF THE SECOND WORLD WAR, BECAME A BOMBER PILOT. HE HAD NUMEROUS ADVENTURES, SURVIVING TWO DITCHINGS IN THE SEA (THUS HIS NICKNAME 'DINGHY') AND WAS TWICE AWARDED THE DISTINGUISHED FLYING CROSS, FOR OPERATIONS OVER GERMANY, ITALY, MALTA AND THE WESTERN DESERT. IN 1942 A POSTING TOOK HIM TO THE USA, WHERE HE MARRIED PRISCILLA RAWSON, WHOM HE HAD KNOWN SINCE HE WAS AT SCHOOL IN AMERICA.

HENRY MELVIN YOUNG, known as Melvin, was born on 20 May 1915 in London. His father, Henry George Melvin Young, was a solicitor serving as a second lieutenant in the Army. His mother was Fannie Forrester Young, formerly Rowan, an American from a socially prominent Los Angeles family. Henry too had studied law at Trinity College, Oxford, where he was a keen oarsman. In 1906 Henry went to the USA and was admitted to the California State Bar and practised law there. Henry and Fannie were married in 1913 and moved to London, where Melvin and his sisters, Mary and Angela, were born.

Melvin was an active and healthy child. He was rather flat footed and was not happy with sports that involved running – he grew to prefer riding and rowing. He was naturally left handed, albeit the educational fashion of the time made him learn to write with his right hand. His handwriting was rather awkward, and it is notable that he preferred to use a typewriter later in life. He had a lifelong habit of sitting cross legged, often on the floor or on a desk.

Melvin Young attended four schools before going up to Trinity College, Oxford: Amesbury School, Hindhead, Surrey, England; Webb School, Claremont, California, USA; Kent School, Connecticut, USA; Westminster School, London, England. He was at school in America from 1928 to 1932; otherwise, apart from visits to the USA and Europe and RAF service abroad, he spent all his life in Britain.

Melvin left small bequests to both Kent and Westminster Schools in his will, and both had a strong influence on his love of rowing. However, it may be said that Kent School had a particular place in his affections, although he was only there from 1930 to 1932. He met his wife at Kent and was married in the school chapel. The school was founded in 1906 by the Revd Frederick Herbert Sill, a man who made a deep impression on generations of his pupils – Melvin continued to correspond with Fr Sill for the rest of his life.

One of Melvin's classmates was Edward (Ed) Rawson, whose family had a house, Ravenscroft Farm, a few miles from Kent School. Melvin came to regard the Rawson household as a home from home, and it was Ed's elder sister, Priscilla, who was destined to become Melvin's wife. Priscilla was a graduate of Bryn Mawr College near Philadelphia. She studied music in England just before the Second World War, and their relationship developed at that time.

Trinity College, Oxford, which Melvin entered in 1934, was basically unchanged, in buildings and ethos, from that to which his father, Henry, came up in 1895. Most of the undergraduates were from professional and landowning families and were confident of their place in the upper reaches of British society. Melvin wrote to Fr Sill a month before he went up to Oxford relating that he had received a letter from his prospective tutor 'giving me a list of books to read this summer, with exams on the second day up'. He confirmed that his family now planned to live in England (no mention of his mother, who was estranged from his father).

Melvin took a major part in rowing at Oxford, first for the college and ultimately for the university against Cambridge. For the college he was in the

Left Melvin riding in California, 1929, probably at Webb School. *(Trinity College, Oxford)*

Left Fannie Rowan competing in the Southern California Tennis Championships, c.1910. She was left handed, as was Melvin. *(Trinity College, Oxford)*

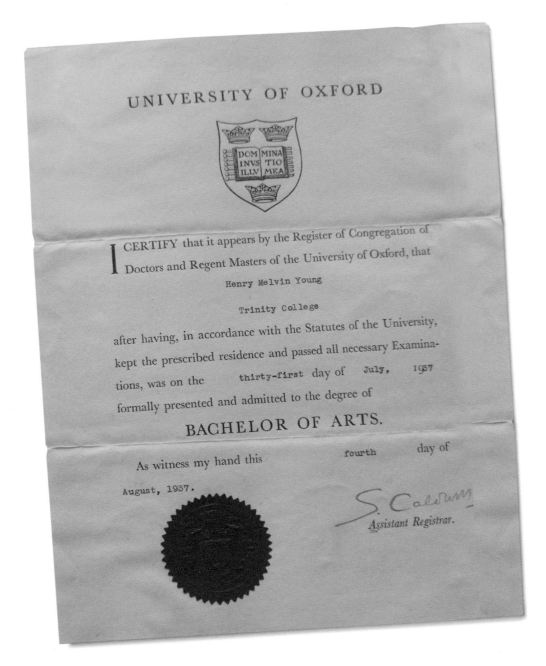

Trinity eight, which became 'Head of the River' in 1938; of the eight oarsmen in that boat, only two survived the Second World War. Four of the eight died serving in the RAF.

Having graduated in 1937 in law, Melvin continued his 'studies' at Trinity and concentrated his efforts of getting a 'Blue', rowing against Cambridge. He did, however, succeed in entering the Oxford University Air Squadron, to satisfy his interest in flying, but it seems that when pressed he gave his time to rowing. The competition to get a place in the Oxford boat was intense.

Melvin rowed in the 1938 University Boat Race, which was given a live broadcast on BBC radio, and was the first to be covered by BBC Television, albeit only in the final stages. Cambridge won the toss and chose the Surrey station. There was rough water from the start and it turned out to be one of the best races for years. For three-quarters of the race the crews were overlapping, but eventually

78

Oxford gained a clear lead and held on to win by two lengths in a time of 20 minutes and 20 seconds.

In 1937 Melvin was accepted into the Oxford University Air Squadron (OUAS). He learned to fly on the Avro Tutor biplane at RAF Abingdon. There are letters on Melvin's OUAS file from which it is clear that he worked hard at combining his flying training with his rowing. In particular he asked for as much 'pre-term' flying as possible immediately after the Boat Race. By the end of the 1938 'Annual Attachment' (summer flying camp) he had flown some forty hours. His instructor was Flight Lieutenant Charles Whitworth (who was to be station commander at Scampton at the time of the Dam Busters raid).

Melvin joined the Royal Air Force Volunteer Reserve (RAFVR) and was commissioned as a Pilot Officer, General Duties Branch, on 13 September 1938. At this time war seemed a real possibility and was eventually declared against Germany on 3 September 1939. On 25 September Melvin reported to No. 1 Initial Training Wing at Cambridge.

The Initial Training Wing would normally have taken eight weeks; however, this was cut to two weeks, and Melvin was posted to No. 9 Service

Left Melvin about to fly an Avro Tutor with the OUAS at the 1938 summer camp. From Priscilla Young's book of press cuttings. *(Trinity College, Oxford)*

Flying Training School at Hullavington in Wiltshire on 7 October 1939. No. 14 Course started that day, with some fourteen officers and eighteen airmen; all were in the RAFVR and were noted as having 'considerable flying experience' – in Melvin's case about a year before!

The syllabus called for eight weeks on the Intermediate Training Squadron (ITS), flying Hart trainers, Audax and Anson aircraft. This was to be followed by eight weeks on the Advanced Training Squadron (ATS), with the addition of the Fury. Unfortunately, the winter weather of 1939/40 was very severe, frequently stopping all movements. All courses were extended; eventually Melvin was posted to RAF Abingdon on 6 April for operational training on the Armstrong Whitworth Whitley bomber.

Melvin was not surprised to be selected as a bomber pilot; indeed, he told his family: 'They won't make me a fighter pilot . . . but maybe just as well, because they only survive three weeks!' However, it is worth recording the Remarks column from his Record of Service under 'Courses of Instruction, etc.':

Left The winning Oxford Boat Race crew, 1938. Melvin is second from left, back row; his close friend Conrad Cherry is holding the trophy. *(Trinity College, Oxford)*

Below left Oxford crew at Putney just before the 1938 Boat Race – Melvin Young is second from bow. Probably taken by his father from a following launch. *(Trinity College, Oxford)*

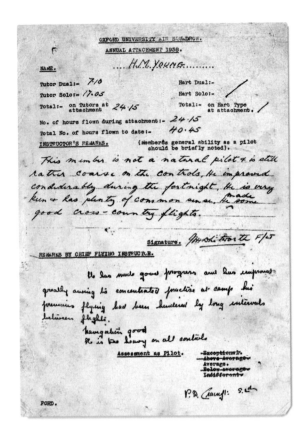

*Flying Training at No. 9 FTS 10/10/39–6/4/40. Ground
subjects above average. An above average pilot attained by
keenness and hard work. General handling of aircraft good.
Should make a good sound service pilot. Above average officer
qualities. A likeable personality and a very satisfactory pupil.
Authorised to wear Flying badge [ie RAF Wings] w.e.f
14/2/40. Passed 79.3%.*

Among Melvin's fellow students at No. 9 SFTS was
Leonard Cheshire. The rest will no doubt have been
from a wide background, albeit all keen enough to
have joined the RAFVR. We have a glimpse of
these other characters from the menu card of the
end-of-course dinner for 'E' Flight, held at the
Cross Hands Hotel at Old Sodbury.

We have some insight into Melvin's religious
feelings at this time. His RAF Record shows him as
being 'Church of England'. In a letter to Fr Sill,
from Hullavington, in March 1940, he says he intended to make his confession, for the first time
since leaving Kent eight years previously, before
taking Easter communion. He said he had been
feeling 'much happier in life recently', although he
was not sure why: 'Whether it being leaving Oxford

or more probably the war I do feel more at peace
with myself in my duty to God.' As an Anglican he
tended towards the 'high church end'. Perhaps it
is no coincidence that Melvin had become a Free-
mason two years earlier; although Freemasonry is
secular, it has abundant rituals and mystic
symbolism.

On 6 April Melvin was posted to No. 10 Operational Training Unit at Abingdon and began
converting on to the Whitley bomber. The 'sharp
end' of the training involved nine days' armament
training at Jurby, on the north-west corner of the
Isle of Man. This training included dive-and-stick-
bombing, low-level attack and defence against
fighters. The weather in that period was excellent,
and the course was busy over the coastal bombing
range, attacking floating targets from various levels,
singly and in formation.

Melvin's first operational posting came on 10 June
1940, to No. 102 (Ceylon) Squadron, No. 4 Group
Bomber Command, based at Driffield. Melvin's
flight commander was Squadron Leader Philip R.
(Teddy) Beare, DFC, with whom Melvin was

destined to serve in the Middle East and who became a firm friend. Leonard Cheshire was also posted to 102 Squadron at this time.

It was standard procedure at that time for newly trained pilots to serve as second pilot for a period in order to familiarize themselves with operations. Thus Melvin's first operational sortie was with Pilot Officer J. F. Painter as his skipper on 19/20 June, attacking marshalling yards at Schwerte, near Dortmund in the Ruhr. After this first raid and up to 24 August, Melvin flew on some thirteen raids with P/O Painter to a range of targets. It was during this period, at the height of the Battle of Britain, that Driffield suffered the heaviest raid on a British bomber station of the entire war, and was put out of action until early in 1941. The raid is well documented elsewhere, but Leonard Cheshire later recalled being in an air-raid shelter with Melvin, who, to relieve the tension, produced a pack of cards and asked, 'Anyone like a game of bridge?' No. 102 Squadron was relocated to Leeming (briefly) and then to Linton-on-Ouse and eventually to Topcliffe.

On 13 August Melvin took part in his first raid on Italy, again with P/O Painter as captain. They reported that enormous fires were started. He later recounted that, when flying over neutral Switzerland 'We could look down and see the homes lighted up in the Swiss towns. It gave us a happy feeling, coming from a land that had been blacked out for a year.'

Back on the ground there was much light-hearted banter in the Mess and some more serious discussion. Melvin sometimes starting involved debates on improbable subjects at a moment's notice. Melvin was a widely read man in whose company Cheshire sparkled, and they provided each other with support in the face of derisive comments about Oxford intellectuals.

On 1 September 1940, No. 102 Squadron moved temporarily to Prestwick, under 15 Group Coastal Command, to provide convoy escort for shipping in the Atlantic. Melvin now became an aircraft commander, and his first operation as such was on 9 September. These flights continued through September, with some aircraft being detached to operate from Aldergrove in Northern Ireland. It was on a flight from Aldergrove, on 7 October 1940, that the first of Melvin's ditchings occurred; the crew consisted of Sergeant Collier (2nd pilot), Pilot Officer Forsdyke, Sergeant Burns and Sergeant Hird. It was a day of moderate to good visibility with a WSW wind up to 20 mph. The Operations Record Book simply records: 'Force landed in sea due-engine trouble. Crew picked up by ex-American destroyer HMS *St Mary's* after 22 hours in dinghy.' Of course there was more to it than this cryptic record tells. Whitleys had a limited single-engine performance and, starting from a low altitude, Melvin found himself and his crew facing a ditching in short order.

This nearly disastrous adventure was well recorded, both in Melvin's own words and by an American reporter, William L. (Bill) White, who was travelling on the destroyer that rescued them. The ship, on its first voyage under the White Ensign as HMS *St Mary's*, was one of the fifty First World War four-funnel, flush-deck destroyers that President Roosevelt agreed to transfer to the Royal Navy. As part of the 'delivery voyage', HMS *St Mary's* and several sister ships provided the surface escort for a convoy. Bill White was able to record the event in words and photographs for the

American public: his report was published in *Life* magazine of 2 December 1940.

Bill White's account of the voyage describes a rough crossing with various alarms because of U-boat activity and aircraft sightings (mostly British, fortunately). Then, off the coast of Northern Ireland, he went to the bridge and found the captain scanning the sea through his binoculars with particular attention. The captain ordered a change of course towards what eventually turned out to be a dinghy containing five people. HMS *St Mary's* was skilfully positioned alongside the dinghy, and the airmen were hauled aboard.

Melvin was photographed with the captain (Lieutenant K. H. J. L. Phibbs), wearing clothes borrowed from Bill White, a splendid publicity photograph for the Admiralty. HMS *St Mary's* was given permission to race on ahead of the convoy to 'a British port' (actually Belfast) with the survivors, who were collected at the dockside by RAF ambulances to take them to hospital for treatment and check-ups, before some well-deserved 'survivors' leave'.

Melvin's own story of the ditching and rescue has survived in various forms, including a radio broadcast at 6pm on the BBC Home Service on

Clockwise, from top left Melvin and his crew in dinghy, 8 October 1940, from HMS *St Mary's*. Another escort vessel stands by; drifting towards HMS *St Mary's*, Melvin with paddle; dinghy alongside, Melvin bottom right, holding line, Sgt Burns (Air Gunner) top left; Melvin with the Captain of HMS *St Mary's* (Lt Phibbs had come out of retirement when war broke out). Note the tired paintwork of this old ship. *(Trinity College, Oxford)*

31 October, entitled 'A Rescue at Sea' by a flying officer (speaking anonymously). He told of descent towards the sea, an SOS sent, a perilous escape from the aircraft into the dinghy, dangerous seas, seasickness, cold, hunger, despair and, eventually, rescue after twenty-two hours.

Back on land, there had been a failure of the rescue alerting system. Later, Melvin stated that 'the woman in the auxiliary at home who caught our [SOS] message somehow put it in the files, and while we all sat in our rubber boat, our distress signal lay resting in a file for future reference'. This is confirmed by a note dated 21 October from Air Vice Marshal Arthur Coningham (AOC-in-C of 4 Group) to Melvin.

On 10 October No. 102 Squadron had returned to No. 4 Group at Linton-on-Ouse. This was the base from which Melvin returned to operations, until 102 moved on to Topcliffe on 16 November. While at Linton, he took part in raids on Bremen, Ruhland, and set off for Berlin on 14 November, but returned after an hour and a half with an unserviceable compass.

From Topcliffe, on 23 November, 102 joined with No. 77 Squadron for a raid on the Royal Arsenal at Turin. The four aircraft from 102 attacked the primary target and the railway station, causing many explosions and large fires. But five Whitleys were lost on this raid, owing to fuel exhaustion – three from 102 and two from 77. Of the 102 aircraft, Sergeant Pearce force-landed near Shoreham, Sergeant Rix and his crew bailed out by parachute near Tangmere, and Melvin ditched off Start Point in Devon; all the 102 crews were saved. Of the two 77 Squadron aircraft, one hit high-tension cables trying to land in Suffolk and the other ditched off Dungeness; its pilot, P/O Bagnel, was rescued, but the remainder of his crew was drowned.

The flying accident card (Air Historical Branch, RAF) tells us that Melvin force-landed DY-F (T4216) in the sea 'due to lack of fuel, having been unable to get a position fix due to an unreliable radio'. The 1942 Ministry of Information booklet

'*Air Sea Rescue*' highlighted this ditching as an ideal rescue. It tells us:

The wireless operator had succeeded in sending an SOS which enabled the Whitley to be plotted some forty miles off Plymouth. There was a slight southerly wind, the sea was calm and there was little moon and no mist. The pilot made a successful tail down landing after switching on his landing lights. The dinghy was inflated without incident. All the crew scrambled aboard, the only mishap being an injury to the tail gunner, who broke his arm when the Whitley hit the water. They entered the dinghy at 4.30 in the morning. They were found by a Lysander, which had gone out at daybreak to search for them, at 10.05 hrs, five hours and thirty-five minutes after ditching. The Lysander approached them with the sun behind it and its pilot saw them easily. The launch arrived at 14.30 hours to pick them up.

Above Letter from Air Marshal Coningham regarding Melvin's ditching. *(Trinity College, Oxford)*

Not surprisingly Melvin then acquired the nickname 'Dinghy' – and sometime later a hoax was perpetrated, supposedly posting him to Calshot to run a dinghy training unit. He had bought a round of drinks in anticipation of leaving 102 Squadron, before finding he was the subject of a prank! It was acknowledged that Melvin had taken all aspects of training very seriously, including dinghy drill, reflecting the personality that had persisted in getting his rowing to a high enough standard to win his Blue at Oxford.

In December Melvin was back in action, raiding targets in Germany, as well as an attack on Merignac (Bordeaux) aimed at the long-range FW200 Condor aircraft, which threatened British convoys in the Atlantic; Melvin attacked from 8,000 feet, putting bombs on the hangars. Melvin's last operation with 102 was to Hanover on 10/11 February 1941.

During this period he was promoted to acting flight lieutenant (15 December 1940), a rank made substantive on 6 April 1941. In May 1941 he was awarded the Distinguished Flying Cross (DFC) for his service with 102 Squadron. The citation, in the *London Gazette* of 9 May 1941 reads:

This officer has carried out 28 bombing missions involving 230 hours flying as well as 6 convoy patrols on which some 40 hours were spent in the air. His operational flights include attacks on important targets in Germany and Italy. On two occasions he has been forced down on the sea, on one of which he was in the dinghy for 22 hours in an Atlantic gale. On both occasions his courage and inspired leadership, combined with a complete knowledge of dinghy drill, were largely responsible for the survival of his crews. He has always shown the greatest keenness to seek out and destroy his targets.

The year 1941 saw many movements for Melvin. Initially he was posted back to No. 10 OTU at RAF Abingdon as an instructor on the Whitley. In April, he was sent to No. 21 OTU at Moreton-in-the-Marsh for a conversion course on the Vickers Wellington bomber. He was at 21 OTU only from 19 to 25 April, just long enough to convert on to the Wellington, despite bad weather and aircraft unserviceability. Melvin was then posted to the newly formed No. 22 OTU equipped with Wellingtons at the new aerodrome at Wellesbourne Mountford, some 4 miles east of Stratford-upon-Avon.

During Melvin's time at Wellesbourne, from April to August 1941, some six courses started: pilots, air observers (navigators), wireless operators/air gunners and air gunners were all trained. Flying training started on 8 May, coinciding with the first attack on the aerodrome by the Luftwaffe. The enemy seemed determined to disrupt the OTU; they attacked again on the 10th and again on the 12th.

The Operations Record Book confirms that rapid strides were made by the Navigation Section, and before his next posting Melvin is recorded as 'Navigation Officer'. The cross-country flights by 'C' Flight (the navigation flight) were reorganized. The majority of night trips used Fishguard (on the

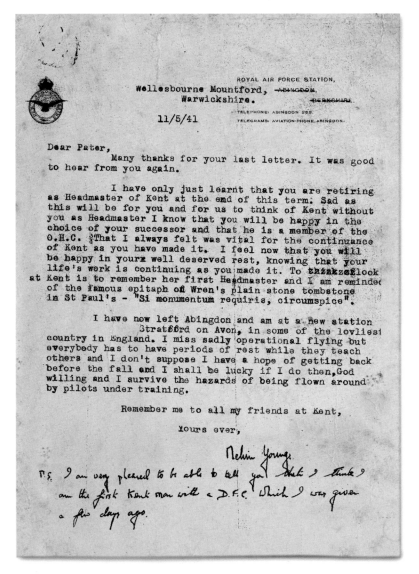

Below Melvin's letter to Father Sill from Wellesbourne Mountford. *(Trinity College, Oxford)*

south-west tip of Wales) as a turning point, 'to enable infra-red photo exercises to be carried out'.

Melvin had mixed feelings about his time teaching new aircrew. But he found time to write to Fr Sill from Wellesbourne Mountford. On 2 September he left Wellesbourne for Driffield, this time to join No. 104 Squadron, for flying duties as a squadron leader, which acting rank he assumed on 7 September.

Melvin's move to No. 104 Squadron put him under the command of Wing Commander P. R. Beare, with whom he had served in No. 102 Squadron. Philip Robert Beare was extremely popular among his colleagues, both junior and senior, being known as 'Teddy Bear' or 'Maxie'; of modest height (5 feet

6 inches), he was of sturdy build and was famous for his 'handlebar' moustache.

Melvin's second period at Driffield was short, because an element of fifteen crews and aircraft from 104 were detached to join No. 238 Wing of No. 205 Group of the Middle East Air Force. On 14 October an advance party under Melvin's command moved to Stanton Harcourt, a satellite aerodrome for Abingdon. A few days later he left for Malta, arriving there without incident on 20 October in company with six other aircraft.

The Wellington bombers were based at Luqa and its satellite 'Safi Strip', the two being connected by a tortuous series of taxiways, off which were located numerous dispersal sites for parked aircraft. The dispersals were given some protection by blast walls made of local stone or sand-filled petrol cans.

The airfields on Malta were subject to concentrated bombing attacks, and many aircraft were lost on the ground as well as to intruding enemy fighters. The Wellington force was needed to attack the ends of the enemy supply lines, at Naples and Tripoli. Malta at that time was described as the most bombed place on earth.

On the night after his arrival, 21 October 1941, Melvin led a force of thirteen aircraft from No. 104 Squadron, accompanied by twelve from 38 Squadron, to attack Naples. On 24 October six Wellingtons led by Philip Beare and Melvin attacked Tripoli. This pattern of raids continued until Christmas. It is notable from the No. 104 Squadron Record Book that during November Melvin started signing the 'Summary of Events' on behalf of Philip Beare. He also performed much routine flying, air tests on air craft after maintenance, 'local' flying including instructing second pilots, and searchlight cooperation.

How they spent Christmas is not recorded, but from his comments the following year we know it was in Malta. Then at the beginning of January 1942 the whole squadron moved to Kabrit in Egypt as part of No. 205 Group, which operated night bombers in the Middle East and Mediterranean theatres of war. Frances Chappell in his book *Wellington Wings* gives us a first-hand account of the operations by No. 104 Squadron at this time. Chappell was a schoolteacher in Dorset in peacetime. In January 1942, at the age of 32, he found himself as a very junior acting pilot officer serving as squadron intelligence officer with 104.

Chappell describes No. 205 Group as 'a smaller Bomber Command . . . a tightly organised and efficient bombing force, flexible enough to be switched in emergency to direct army support in attacking enemy tanks, transport and troops close to the front line'. He continues:

Operating conditions for the men of these night bomber squadrons were very different from the conditions prevailing for Bomber Command crews in Europe. The No. 205 Group Squadrons were units of a mobile bomber force based in

Left
No. 104 Squadron, Rolls-Royce Merlin-engined Wellington II, Egypt 1942. W/Cdr Philip Beare, centre, with Melvin on his right and S/Ldr Brown on his left. *(Trinity College, Oxford)*

Right Letter from
Air Marshal Tedder
regarding the 1942
detachment to Malta.
(Trinity College, Oxford)

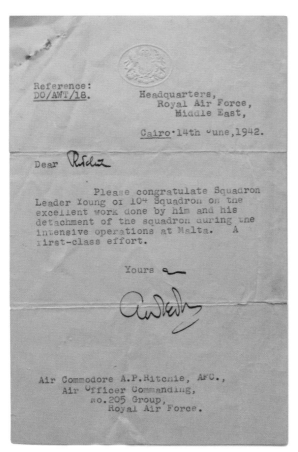

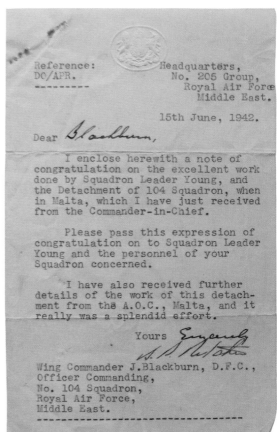

*tents, trucks and improvised runways scraped from the desert
surface . . . airfield equipment was primitive, maintenance of
engines and airframes difficult, living conditions always
uncomfortable, 'gippy tummy' was common, relaxation in
cities with music, dancing and female company was rare
indeed; rising sand and dust storms, hot humid days and
freezing nights were part of the environment . . . on the happier
side, weather conditions were settled for longer periods and
targets were usually less heavily defended than in Germany
and losses on normal missions were lower than for Bomber
Command. Exceptions were the 'Mail Run', regular targets
frequently attacked, such as Benghazi and Tobruk.*

RAF Station Kabrit, near the Great Bitter Lakes
on the Suez Canal, was the home base for two
Wellington squadrons, 104 and 148. Chappell records
that 104 had 'expected to return to Britain after
their detachment to Malta. Instead, the surviving
aircraft and crews were posted to the Middle East
to reinforce the 205 Group force of night bombers.'
No. 104 Squadron was formed of two flights, under
Melvin and Squadron Leader D. J. Brown, DFC,

using additional new crews from 205 Group.

In order to increase the bomb load or range of
the Wellingtons, use was made of Advanced
Landing Grounds (ALGs) in the Daba area. In particular, 236 Wing used LG 106, some 20 miles west
of El Alamein, and sometimes LG 109 (Bir
Koraiyim) a few miles further west. The aircraft were
bombed up at Kabrit and fuelled to reach Daba
with a reserve to return if necessary. At the ALG
the aircraft were refuelled for the operation and
the crews given last-minute meteorological and
intelligence briefings. On returning from the
missions, the aircraft landed at the ALG for an intelligence debriefing before flying back to Kabrit.
Eventually it was decided to move the Wellington
squadrons into the desert landing grounds, and this
happened in May for 104.

Chappell clearly had great respect for Melvin's
record and leadership but sometimes was disturbed
by his manner; for instance, on 13 March at ALG
106 Chappell records: 'At the briefing by Squadron
Leader Young he shut me out entirely. He is a large

and formidable man with great experience and fame as a courageous bomber pilot but seems impatient with non-flying types such as IOs [Intelligence Officers]. I can understand this.' These comments by Chappell are among the few that describe Melvin as anything other than amiable. Melvin later commented in a speech at Kent School how disagreeable he found the heat, sand and flies in Egypt, and no doubt the conditions and the stresses of war made everyone tense. However, Chappell also describes Melvin as 'selfless in his complete devotion to the task of bombing efficiently'.

At one period, 6 to 16 April 1942, extra responsibility was placed on Melvin as Philip Beare was away inspecting landing grounds in Palestine and Syria. In addition to operational flying there were instructional flights, circuits and landings with second pilots, air tests and searchlight cooperation. Photographs from this period show that Melvin had grown a neat moustache. Notably, a few months later, he was clean shaven again.

From ALG 106 on 23 May Melvin led a detachment of ten 104 Squadron Wellingtons, with twenty key maintenance personnel, five additional crews and certain heavy bombs, back to Malta for a period of intensive operations. Between 1 and 10 June they carried out eight operations against the Augusta Submarine base, Cagliari, Catania aerodrome (twice), Naples harbour and Taranto harbour (three times).

This detachment resulted in a note, addressed to Air Commodore A. P. Ritchie, AFC, AOC 205 Group (and passed on to Wing Commander Blackburn, now the commanding officer of 104) from Air Marshal Tedder, the Commander-in-Chief RAF Middle East.

Melvin's tour with No. 104 Squadron resulted in his being gazetted, on 18 September 1942, for a Bar to his DFC. The citation was presented to Priscilla Young at the British Embassy in Washington in 1944.

In the RAF Museum Library there is a collection of papers left by Group Captain Philip Beare. Among them is a poignant manuscript letter from Priscilla Young, written after Melvin's death. She congratulates Philip on the Bar to his DSO and says that Melvin had been 'terribly pleased to get his DFC Bar last year and felt that he owed it entirely to your kind words'. She went on to comment:

Melvin was apt to lack confidence in his own abilities and the only way in which he could gain assurance was to tackle some hard job. I feel the responsibility you gave him proved of invaluable help. I know he thought you let him take more responsibility than, as a Squadron Leader, he might otherwise have had.

Priscilla ends her letter: 'I could see that Melvin had grown up a great deal during his year in Egypt and I should like to say "thank you" for all the help you gave him.'

Melvin now had a brief period at HQ 205 Group before he was posted to the RAF Delegation in Washington DC to take up temporary duties from 2 September with the United States Army Air Corps. On 24 July he started a long, tiring journey to the USA.

This route was a well-used ferry route for aircraft and personnel to and from Egypt and the USA, via West Africa and South America. The flight set from Heliopolis (Cairo) to Wadi Seidna. The next day took them first to El Fasher in the Sudan, and then on to Kano. The two following days took them via Lagos and Accra to Robertsfield in Liberia and a short transfer to Fish Lake, where they embarked in a PanAm Clipper flying boat for an overnight eleven-hour flight to Natal on the extreme eastern coastline of Brazil. There they had a brief stop before continuing to Belem and thereafter via British

Below Melvin's British Forces ID card, Egypt March 1942 (left) and his 1942 passport photo (right), shortly before departure to USA, now clean shaven and notably more relaxed. *(Trinity College, Oxford)*

Name **YOUNG Henry Melvin**
Description **Squadron Leader**
Unit **Royal Air Force**
Height **6' 1"**
Colour of Eyes **Blue**
Colour of Hair **Brown**
Signature of Holder

Right Melvin and Priscilla with her parents, Clementine and Hobart Rawson at Ravenscroft Farm, 10 August 1942. *(Trinity College, Oxford)*

Guiana, Trinidad, Puerto Rico, Miami and eventually to Washington DC. In a letter to his mother, Melvin commented that he had taken eight days flying to the USA from Egypt, having arrived at the end of July, and was very tired.

On Saturday, 1 August 1942, Melvin telephoned his mother Fannie, in California, from New York City. He followed this with a short letter in which he told her that he had met some of the Rawsons and would be 'off to Kent at the crack of dawn to see the rest of the Rawson family and have a few days rest there and see the school again'. His arrival at Ravenscroft Farm, on Sunday, 2 August, was indeed early in the morning. By lunchtime, Melvin had proposed marriage to Priscilla. Although they had known each other for many years, were good friends, enjoyed each other's company and conversation and had spent time together in both the USA and England, this took Priscilla completely by surprise. She took a deep breath and two days before deciding to accept Melvin's proposal. Priscilla was a well-educated, well-travelled young woman, with a considerable knowledge of literature and music, but she was never much interested in matters of fashion or glamour; she was somewhat

above average height, slim and rather short-sighted. She had an independent income and no need of a husband to support her. Like Melvin, she enjoyed riding, and there was plenty of scope for this at Ravenscroft. He warned Priscilla that his duties in the RAF had been very hazardous and would probably be so again. Nonetheless, he wanted very much to get married, and she was the lady of his choice.

The day of Monday, 10 August, was chosen for the wedding, to be held in the Chapel at Kent School with a reception at Ravenscroft Farm afterwards. The new headmaster of Kent, Father Chalmers, OHC, agreed to officiate. Melvin sent the surprise news of his forthcoming marriage via his Aunt Floss, asking her to 'break the news gently' to his mother. He was relieved to receive a cable in return to say that Fannie was very happy. The news was sweetened for Fannie because Melvin and Priscilla were to fly to Los Angeles immediately after the wedding.

This wartime wedding was a relatively small affair – most young men were away in the services and the location of the reception at Ravenscroft is somewhat remote. Ed Rawson, as a long-time friend, acted as best man, becoming brother-in-law as the ceremony progressed.

The newly-weds were then driven to New York to catch the 8.30pm (Eastern Time) TWA 'Sky Chief' Flight 7 to Los Angeles. This service, using Douglas DC-3 aircraft, made stops at Pittsburgh, Chicago, Kansas City, Amarillo, and Albuquerque and was due to arrive at Los Angeles, Burbank Airport, at 11.33am, Pacific Time. This was Priscilla's first ever flight in any aircraft and was a very tiring introduction to the air. Melvin, by contrast, had plenty of opportunity to compare notes with the TWA pilots.

On arrival at Burbank, Melvin and Priscilla were met by Fannie and Aunt Floss, who had offered the newly-weds the use of her ranch, Cielito Lindo, which Melvin knew well, and the family cabin on Great Bear Lake, high up in the San Bernardino Mountains. The 'cabin', actually quite a substantial house, was in a picturesque setting perhaps 100 feet above the lake. This was certainly a very romantic place for a honeymoon. All good things must come to an end, and soon enough it was time to return to

Left Melvin's tour with No. 104 Squadron resulted in his being gazetted, on 18 September 1942, for a Bar to his DFC. The citation is as presented to Priscilla Young at the British Embassy in Washington in 1944. (*Trinity College, Oxford*)

SQUADRON LEADER HENRY M. YOUNG

Bar to Distinguished Flying Cross

This officer participated in the first
large scale attack on Naples, pressing home his
attack with great determination. On another
occasion, when returning to Malta from a raid
on Tripoli, a stick of bombs burst on the airfield
while Squadron Leader Young was landing his aircraft,
setting fire to a bomb loaded aircraft. Displaying
great coolness, he completed his landing and
avoided obstructions on the runway. He dispersed
his aircraft, then took charge of the flare path
and had it moved so that the remainder of the squadron
were enabled to land.

London Gazette dated 18.9.42.

BRITISH EMBASSY
WASHINGTON, D.C.
13th June, 1944.

the East Coast. On the way back Melvin and Priscilla broke their journey at Albuquerque, New Mexico, and enjoyed a brief visit to the mountains in that state.

On 31 August Melvin and Priscilla set off for Washington DC. Melvin was now to spend two weeks in Florida giving talks to the US Army Air Corps.

His next posting was to the Twin-Engined Advanced Flying Training School at Turner Field, Albany, Georgia, where RAF pilots developed their skills. Records show that the Turner Field Advanced School achieved graduation rates around 90 per cent for the period when Melvin was there.

Right Melvin Young addressing an audience in the USA, 1942. (*Trinity College, Oxford*)

Significantly, no trainees were killed – probably a reflection of operating in better weather conditions than would have been the case in Britain. Priscilla was able to accompany Melvin on this posting to Georgia and took part in the social life at the airbase.

Melvin wrote to Fr Chalmers at Kent on 17 January 1943 telling him that he and Priscilla had a 'very quiet Christmas'. He explained the tradition in the British Services that officers serve the men dinner on Christmas day: 'An enormous meal was provided and the RAF Officers helped wait at table and served beer to the cadets. It seemed a far cry to my last Christmas spent in Malta.'

Melvin explained to Fr Chalmers that he had been kept very busy at Turner Field, with the title of RAF Liaison Officer, giving some lectures and doing quite a lot of flying instruction. However, 'the last of the British cadets training under the Arnold scheme leave next month and my job will be ending in a few weeks' time'. Indeed, within two

weeks he was on his way to England, to bomber operations. Melvin ended his letter by asking Fr Chalmers to be the first American recipient should any bad news be sent by his father and to break it to the Rawson family, and Priscilla in particular, as he (Fr Chalmers) saw fit. Melvin said his final goodbye to Priscilla in New York on 2 February 1943 (the end of their married life together) and set off by train to Boston on the first stage of his journey to England.

Melvin had at this time been away from operations over northern Europe for some two years (excepting a very limited period with 104 Squadron at Driffield in October 1941) and had yet to be introduced to the heavy four-engined bombers such as the Avro Lancaster. This introduction came in the first half of March at 1654 Conversion Unit (CU), Wigsley, and 1660 CU, Swinderby. It seems likely that Melvin met his crew at 1660 CU at Swinderby.

On 13 March Melvin and his new crew were posted to 57 Squadron at Scampton, with Melvin in command of 'C' Flight. Before Melvin could take part in any operations with 57 Squadron, he was caught up in the urgent formation of a new squadron, which was to undertake a special operation and then be available for other unusual bombing tasks. The new squadron was soon allocated the now famous number 617, and 'C' Flight of 57 Squadron was posted in toto across the station on 25 March. These 'C' Flight crews were led by Melvin, Flight Lieutenant William (Bill) Astell, Pilot Officer Geoff Rice and Flight Sergeant Ray Lovell. They had not volunteered for this unknown assignment; Rice protested but to no avail. Lovell was posted back to 57 Squadron after two weeks: 'The crew did not come up to the standards necessary for this squadron.'

Melvin's original crew were all sergeants:

David Horsfall:	Flight engineer
Charles Roberts:	Navigator
Lawrence Nichols:	Wireless operator
Gordon Yeo:	Air gunner
Wilfred Ibbotson:	Air gunner

The original bomb aimer was John Beesley, but for some reason he was judged unsuitable for 617

Squadron and a Canadian, Flying Officer Vincent MacCausland, was drafted into the crew.

Given Melvin's experience of administration and training, it was natural that he should have been made one of the two flight commanders. He was to take much of the load from Gibson in organizing the heavy training programme that was necessary. Indeed, Gibson wrote in *Enemy Coast Ahead* that 'Melvyn [sic] had been responsible for a good deal of the training which made this raid possible. He had endeared himself to the boys.' Geoff Rice remarked of Melvin: 'He lived with a typewriter, a fantastic administrator.' Gibson also wrote that Melvin could down a pint of beer faster than anyone if he chose to do so.

Melvin's crew averaged over 27 years of age, which was old for aircrew. Three of them, including Melvin, were married. Most of them had very little operational experience (and that gained at the Conversion Unit), and it must be a tribute to Melvin's determined attitude to training that, when tested on Operation Chastise, they performed well. In a letter to his parents a few days before the operation, Gordon Yeo wrote: 'You say you want to know the name of our skipper, well here it is, S/Ldr H. M. Young, he is not so bad lately, I expect that is because we are getting used to him, but he is the cause more or less for us not getting leave.' Writing to Philip Beare after the raid, Priscilla said of Melvin: 'He did speak of the especially good type of boy he had in his flight and of how much he liked his new squadron.'

From early in April Melvin and his crew started flying in earnest. There were many bombing runs, using small practice bombs, at the Wainfleet range and cross-country exercises. On 5 April Melvin and his crew did a five-hour flight, routing Stafford, Lake Vyrnwy, Caldey Island (Pembrokeshire), Wells (Somerset), Hunstanton (Norfolk), Wainfleet and back to Scampton. Gordon Yeo, who came from Barry in south Wales, wrote to his parents: 'We have just come back from a trip of five hours. We were flying quite close to Barry this morning. We flew right down the coast and came back round Cornwall and Bridgwater – a lovely trip. We were flying in our shirt sleeves half the time as it was so hot.'

Above Melvin's will, showing his father as his executor. (*Trinity College, Oxford*)

There were also various technical flights to be performed. One day Melvin took an aircraft to Waddington to be fitted with 'two-stage amber', a blue transparency fitted to the Perspex in two of the Lancasters to be used in conjunction with yellow goggles to simulate moonlight conditions in daytime. Throughout April Melvin managed to fly some thirty-seven hours, but thirty-two of these were in daytime. By the time of the raid he had accumulated only sixty hours since the squadron had been formed, of which twenty-one were at night, including 'spotlight runs' and cross-country flights.

On 9 May Melvin and Henry Maudslay flew their aircraft in company to test newly fitted VHF radio telephone (R/T) sets. These VHF sets had been installed to enable adequate voice communication between aircraft captains, so that they could control the attack on the dams. Radio silence would be maintained as far as possible and essential communications with 5 Group HQ would be by wireless/ telegraphy (W/T). However, it had soon become clear that tactical control around the dams would need voice control, so these VHF sets were fitted.

On Monday, 10 May, Melvin signed a new will, witnessed by his father, Henry. On this document Melvin's address was given as that of his father, 117 Fore St, Hertford, a flat above Henry's office. As a recently married man returning to active service, it would have been important for Melvin to make this will. Guy Gibson had also urged his officers to ensure that their wills were up to date – a strong hint that the forthcoming operation would be hazardous.

On 11 May Melvin flew a cross-country route in formation with the aircraft of Maltby and Shannon, with whom he would be flying en route to the dams. From 11 to 13 May various aircraft from 617 flew to Reculver and dropped inert Upkeep weapons towards the beach.

Later on 14 May a 'dress rehearsal operation' was flown via the lakes at Uppingham and Abberton, which Gibson noted as 'completely successful'. All was set for Operation Chastise. Also on 13 May Melvin wrote what was to be his last letter to Priscilla. In this letter he spoke of certain plans he had made, which indicated that he expected to go on an operation shortly. He was worried because Priscilla had a medical condition that might soon require the need for surgery.

On 15 May the Executive Order for Operation Chastise was issued: the raid was to be flown the next night, 16/17 May. The weather forecast was good, and the moon (which was full in the period 17–20 May) would rise at 1700 and set at 0431 (all times in British Double Summer Time, GMT plus two hours). During the afternoon of 15 May, Barnes Wallis was flown to Scampton, and Melvin was called to a meeting at the Station Commander's house. At this meeting, Melvin, Henry Maudslay ('B' Flight commander), John Hopgood (who had been selected to be deputy leader for the attack on the Möhne Dam) and Flight Lieutenant Bob Hay, who was the squadron's bombing leader, were briefed by Wallis and Gibson on the targets, the details of the weapon and its delivery. Such was the level of security that the rest of the aircrews were not told until the pre-raid briefing on 16 May, when models of the Möhne and Sorpe Dams were available for inspection as well as photographs of the other targets. This full briefing, principally by Wallis and Gibson, was very thorough and caused considerable excitement, and possibly some relief that it was not to be the battleship *Tirpitz*.

The Operational Executive Order required that the raid be flown at low level, not above 500 feet, except between Ahlen (the final waypoint) and the target, where the leader of each section should

Right
German photograph of Lancaster wreckage on the Dutch beach, thought to be AJ-A. (*TNA Air 20/4367*)

climb to 1,000 feet 10 miles from the target (presumably to ensure finding the target with certainty). After the raid Maltby and Shannon commented that Melvin had shown a tendency to fly higher than them, and they had used Aldis signal lamps to warn him to keep low. For his part he would have been feeling a great responsibility to lead his team accurately. It may also be that, with relatively little recent flying, on his first operation in a Lancaster and his first for nearly a year, and with a crew with little operational experience, he was more concerned about hitting obstacles on the ground than they were.

It is fortunate that the navigation log of Sergeant V. Nicholson, in David Maltby's AJ-J, has survived, and so the progress of Melvin's section of three aircraft is well described. Over the Wash they let down low enough to test the spotlights on the water, calibrating the aircraft's pressure altimeters in the process. Their route took them to Southwold with its distinctive lighthouse, and this was to be the last sight of Britain for Melvin and his crew in AJ-A.

They were then over the North Sea, with only a very small change of track to their next waypoint at the mouth of the river Scheldt in Holland. At this point the bomb aimers armed the self-destructive fuses in the Upkeep weapons.

Now began the difficult task of flying low over enemy territory and finding the way, while avoiding obstacles such as power lines and pylons – both the front gunner and the bomb aimer had a literally vital role in looking out for such hazards and warning the pilot to pull up in good time. The route had been chosen with easily identifiable waypoints and reasonably short distances between them, avoiding known flak concentrations as far as possible.

Coming to the somewhat more hilly country approaching the Möhne, Melvin would have climbed AJ-A to make sure he could see the lake in good time. Nicholson's log records that they now switched on their VHF radio sets and started circling (in prearranged locations), and commented that the 'flak [was] none too light'. They had arrived at the principal target. In Gibson's words: 'As we came over the hill, we saw the Möhne Lake. Then we saw the dam itself. In that light it looked

squat and heavy and unconquerable; it looked grey and solid in the moonlight as though it were part of the countryside itself and just as immovable.'

The geography of the dam and the performance of the aircraft made it necessary to attack the dam by lining up over the southern arm of the lake, diving and descending along the slope of the Heversberg Peninsula just above the trees, gaining the necessary speed (220 mph) to release the weapon. Indeed, Gibson's account tells us that his bomb aimer warned him: 'You're going to hit those trees.' However, it was indeed necessary to get down to the bombing height as early as possible in the run: this author's calculations show that, if the aircraft was levelled off 1,650 yards from the dam (the shore is only 1,900 yards out), then at 220 mph there would be only eleven seconds before reaching the release point at 450 yards – not much time, but just enough for a well-trained, determined crew. In this short time the height had to be settled at 60 feet and the line adjusted to aim at the centre of the dam, with the wings level.

The engine throttles would have been adjusted by the flight engineer to maintain the speed gained in the dive. In addition to the noise and vibration from the engines and propellers (high enough anyway), there would have been the added vibration, with a different frequency and amplitude, of the weapon rotating at 500 rpm. Although the weapons were balanced as well as possible, it was reported that they did cause a noticeable vibration.

The tactic was to be that Gibson would attack first, with the others orbiting at low altitude in agreed positions nearby. They would come in to attack in turn at the leader's command; he would call them on VHF using the call sign 'Cooler', with a number denoting their position in the order of action – thus AJ-A would be 'Cooler 4'.

After unsuccessful attempts by Gibson, Hopgood and Martin at 0043, Melvin and his crew made their attempt. Melvin would have climbed AJ-A from its holding orbit to a height that practice had told him would be enough to achieve 220 mph after a shallow dive with the weapon on. He visually lined up with the centre of the dam and pushed the nose down to gain speed and followed the contours of the Heversberg Peninsula as closely as he dared.

Right Remembrance scroll from King and Country. *(Trinity College, Oxford)*

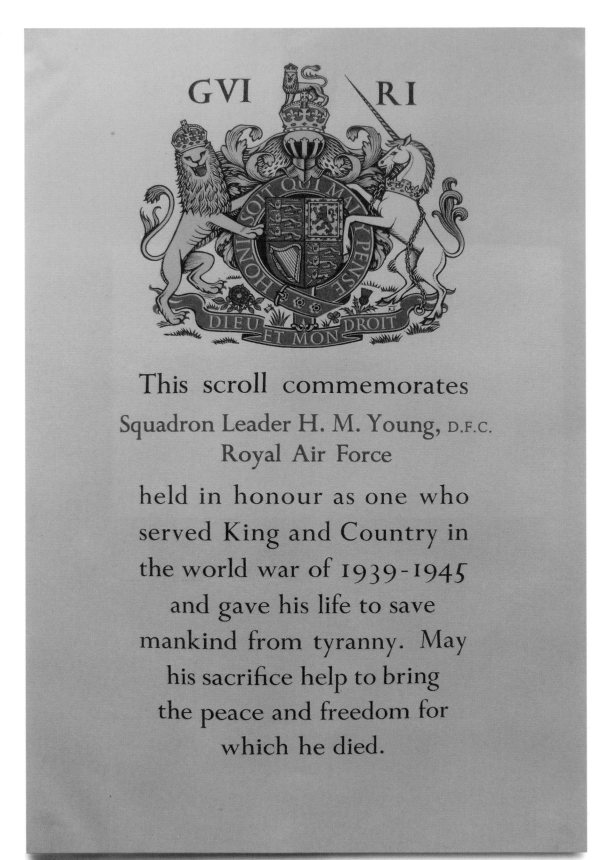

GVI RI

This scroll commemorates

Squadron Leader H. M. Young, D.F.C.
Royal Air Force

held in honour as one who
served King and Country in
the world war of 1939-1945
and gave his life to save
mankind from tyranny. May
his sacrifice help to bring
the peace and freedom for
which he died.

Meanwhile, Larry Nichols, the wireless operator, had checked that the weapon was rotating at 500 rpm, and Charles Roberts, the navigator, had switched on the spotlights and positioned himself by the starboard blister in the cockpit canopy in order to give Melvin up/down guidance over the water surface. David Horsfall, the flight engineer, controlled the engine throttles and kept a close watch on the air-speed indicator, aiming to have the speed at 220 mph as they levelled over the lake and pushing the levers forward as necessary to maintain that speed. The air gunners, Gordon Yeo and Wilfred Ibbotson, prepared to engage the defences – all the squadron guns were loaded with tracer ammunition the better to assess their aim and, hopefully, frighten the enemy. Gibson, whose leadership throughout can only be described as heroic, was now flying on the air side of the dam to distract the enemy gunners and Martin flew in alongside AJ-A to draw some of the flak.

After its release, the weapon fell further behind the aircraft with each bounce and the rear gunner could see the plumes of spray. Gibson recorded that Young's weapon made 'three good bounces and contact' with the dam. It sank to its pre-set depth and exploded against the dam wall, as Wallis had predicted. Another huge column of water rose and a shock wave could be seen rippling through the lake. Melvin glanced back and thought he must have broken it, but in fact later analysis indicated that the dam was now beginning to break but it did not collapse immediately. And so Nichols sent a wireless signal to HQ saying they had hit the dam but it was unbroken.

It was now David Maltby's turn to attack in AJ-J at 0049. Gibson and Martin orbited on the water side of the dam, engaging the flak positions (some of which had now been silenced) to take the heat off AJ-J. As Maltby raced in, he saw that 'the crown of the wall was already crumbling . . . a tremendous amount of debris on the top . . . a breach in the centre of the dam'. With admirable presence of mind in the time available, he adjusted his line slightly left and his weapon was released, making four bounces, struck the dam, sank and exploded. It was not immediately obvious that the dam was now broken. When the spray had subsided, Gibson could see that a great gap, some 150 metres long had appeared in the dam and a torrent of water

surged down the valley below, 'looking like stirred porridge in the moonlight'. Thus about forty minutes after Gibson had reached the Möhne, the code word 'Nigger' was transmitted by Gibson's wireless operator, at 0056. This was received at 5 Group HQ and the excitement there equalled that over the Möhne.

There were now only three aircraft of the second wave armed with Upkeep: AJ-Z (Maudslay), AJ-L (Shannon) and AJ-N (Knight). Conscious of the time, Gibson sent Martin and Maltby home and, with Melvin as his deputy, led the three armed aircraft towards the Eder Dam. The Eder Dam was not defended by guns, but it was in very difficult terrain. It took the three attacking aircraft eleven attempts to launch their weapons, the last of which dropped by Knight was successful. Melvin's role at the Eder was a watching brief, ready to take over from Gibson if necessary.

The aircraft over the Eder now had a strong incentive to get home safely and as quickly as possible. Three return routes had been specified in the operational order; all involved retracing the route via the Möhne Dam, Ahlen and the lakes at Dulmen. From Dulmen there was some choice, but all routes involved crossing the Ijsselmeer (Zuider Zee) and the Helder Peninsula in north Holland. Melvin and Guy Gibson seem to have chosen the most southerly route, which continued back to the same crossing point on the Rhine at Rees, then north-west to near Harderwijk on the Ijsselmeer, and on to leave the Dutch North Sea coast at a known 'gap' in the defences near Egmond. They set course from the Eder at approximately 0155 and, given that Melvin seems to have reached the North Sea in a few minutes over one hour, he must have averaged a speed of about 215 mph – full-throttle all the way and as low as possible.

The general advice was to cross the coast as fast and as low as possible. Two of the pilots, Gibson and Shannon, climbed quite high (800 feet according to Shannon) a few miles before the coast and crossed it in a full-throttle dive, judging the flight path to give the guns the least chance of success.

Sadly, in the case of Melvin Young and his crew, the guns did score a success. At 0258 gunners at Castricum-an-Zee reported shooting down an aircraft (almost certainly Melvin's Lancaster), and several batteries also reported firing at it. AJ-A crashed into the sea, and all its crew were killed.

It will never be known whether Melvin crossed the coast too high, or too near IJmuiden – his inexperienced navigator, Charles Roberts, aided by Vincent MacCausland map reading in the nose of the aircraft, seem to have done an admirable job of helping their captain find the way previously. Melvin had demonstrated at the Möhne Dam that he had become a very accomplished pilot, and had trained his crew well. Nonetheless, one hit with a high-explosive shell had a good chance of destroying an aircraft, and so it was. Whatever the reason, their luck had deserted them at the last hurdle, and thus ended their historic and heroic last night.

Immediately after the raid it was Gibson's duty to write to the next of kin of the fifty-six men who had not returned from the raid, to tell them that their loved one was missing, and to express hope that they had survived and would be reported as prisoners of war. In Melvin's case he had nominated his father as next of kin. This is the letter sent by Gibson to Henry Young:

My dear Mr Young,

It is with deep regret that I write to confirm my telegram advising you that your son, Squadron Leader Henry Melvin Young DFC, is missing as a result of operations.

Squadron Leader Young was a great personal friend of mine and was himself largely responsible for the success of this operation. He was deputy leader of this raid and I watched him drop his load in exactly the right position with great precision. Afterwards we led the raid on the Eder Dam and he and I flew on the return journey back to base. Somewhere, however, between the target and the enemy coast he ran into trouble and has not returned.

If as is possible your son was able to abandon his aircraft and land safely in enemy territory, news should reach you direct from the International Red Cross Committee within the next six weeks. Please accept my sincere sympathy during this anxious period of waiting.

I have arranged for his personal effects to be taken care of by the Committee of Adjustment Officer and these will be forwarded to you through the normal channels in due course.

If there is any way in which I can help you please let me know.

Yours sincerely (signed by Guy Gibson).

A total of thirty-four awards were made to surviving aircrew, including Gibson's Victoria Cross. Five of the pilots were awarded the next most distinguished award for gallantry, the Distinguished Service Order (DSO). Had they survived, the two flight commanders, Melvin Young and Henry Maudslay, would undoubtedly have received the DSO; but, unlike the VC, this award is not made posthumously.

As May wore on, the North Sea gave up the bodies of Melvin and his crew. They were washed ashore by the tides some miles to the north of where they crashed and are buried in the General Cemetery of the nearest small town, Bergen, north Holland. Five of them are buried side by side; Melvin's grave is in the centre of this group, with Vincent MacCausland and Gordon Yeo on his right and David Horsfall and Wilfred Ibbotson to his left. The bodies of Charles Roberts and Lawrence Nichols were recovered later and are buried separately, but near by. Altogether some 250 Allied airmen are buried in this cemetery. Fresh flowers are placed regularly by each grave of Melvin's crew by two local people, Jan van Dalen and his daughter Marielle ('Macy') Plugge-van Dalen.

Among German records is a photograph of the wreckage of a Lancaster on the beach near Bergen from the same period; it is not certain that this was AJ-A, but it seems likely that it was.

It was not until August that the family finally

Right
Macy and Jan van Dalen, who regularly place flowers by Melvin's grave. Macy is a keen student of Dam Buster history.
(Macy van Dalen)

received confirmation that Melvin had been killed and was buried in Holland. This sad news at least enabled them, on both sides of the Atlantic, to take steps to tidy up his affairs and organise memorial services. In Connecticut it was arranged that a service was held in the Kent School Chapel on Sunday evening, 17 October, at 6pm.

A few weeks later, on Monday, 20 December, a joint memorial service was held for Melvin and his good friend Conrad Cherry, who had died when HMS *Welshman* was sunk on 1 February 1943. The service was held at 2pm in St Margaret's Westminster, appropriately for two students from Westminster School. After Psalm 121 and the lesson from Wisdom III, 1–9, came Sir Cecil Spring Rice's famous, and entirely appropriate, hymn:

I vow to thee, my Country, all earthly things above,
Entire and whole and perfect, the service of my love;
The love that asks no question, the love that stands the test,
That lays upon the Altar the dearest and the best

 . . . . .

And soul by soul and silently her shining bounds increase,
And her ways are ways of gentleness and all her paths are peace.

Then after prayers the service ended with another hymn, followed by the benediction.

In January 1944 Melvin's last will (dated 10 May 1943, a week before his death) was granted probate with his father, Henry, as sole executor. Melvin's estate amounted to £4,433 18 shillings and 10 pence – not a fortune but a substantial sum, which would have been enough to buy a comfortable house at that time.

Thus Henry Young had the task, not uncommon during the war, of acting as executor of his son's estate. Henry would have been guided by Melvin's letter, written at the start of the war and to be opened on his death. The letter ends: 'Don't be sad that I am dead: I am at last happy . . . with all my love from your devoted son, Melvin.'

Also early in 1944 Priscilla received Melvin's personal effects, including a 'goodbye', handwritten letter from him. She was just about to leave Ravenscroft for Boston, where she had found a job that would take her mind off her loss. Fortunately the letter came while she was still at home with her mother; Clementine Rawson recorded that 'it was the most beautiful letter full of love, hope and happiness'.

Four months later, on Tuesday, 13 June, Priscilla was in Washington to receive the Bar to Melvin's DFC from the hands of the British Ambassador, Lord Halifax. The ceremony was held in the ballroom of the Embassy.

Later still she received the impressive scroll, decorated with the Royal Coat of Arms, 'Sent by Command of the King', as posted to the families of all who had lost their lives in the service of their country.

Priscilla Rawson Young did not marry again. She spent most of her long life –she died in 2000 aged 91 – in Boston, where she worked in support of local orchestras, a classical music radio station and her favourite charities, which she was able to help financially. She also passed much time at Ravenscroft, especially when her parents were getting old, and is buried nearby in the Skiff Mountain churchyard.

There are numerous memorials on which Melvin is commemorated: at Trinity College, Oxford; at Webb School and Kent School in the USA; at Westminster School in London; at the Kingston Rowing Club.

Arguably the least conventional, but best-known, memorial to Melvin and all his colleagues on Operation Chastise is the 1955 feature film *The Dam Busters*. Made in black and white, thus re-creating the mood of wartime newsreels, it might be described as a 'dramatized documentary'. Guy Gibson was played by Richard Todd and Melvin by Richard Leech. Because of this film, Melvin is probably better known to history by his nickname 'Dinghy'. The film helped to make Operation Chastise one of the most famous raids in the history of the RAF. One poignant scene, after the raid, purports to show the blade from his Boat Race oar on the wall of his room at Scampton. ●

Above
Melvin's 'Boat Race' oar. (*David Young*)

Dam Buster Henry Melvin Young rests with his crew at Bergen General Cemetery, North Holland. Of the 247 Second World War Commonwealth burials, most are airmen and 34 are unidentified. In addition 13 Polish airmen are also at rest. *(Fighting High)*

POSTSCRIPT

BY ROBERT OWEN

THE INTERVENING YEARS have seen revisionists question the effects and the value of Operation Chastise. They argue that the outcome of the operation were far less than protagonists claim, that destruction of the targets was of little consequence to the German war effort and that Upkeep could hardly be considered a successful weapon, since it was never used again. Yet the operation has withstood their attempts to reduce it to the level of an expensive sideshow. Is it that the mythmakers of wartime propaganda along with the journalistic authors and patriotic film-makers of the 1950s did too good a job – or is it that beyond their hyperbole the results of Chastise, both direct and indirect, fully justified the effort, resource and sacrifice the operation demanded?

The truth is that the Dams Raid is a victim of its own propaganda. Initial press reports of the operation were fuelled by an orchestrated public-relations campaign, including the utilization of a royal visit, investiture en masse and Wing Commander Gibson's tour of North America. The propaganda was for both Allied and Axis consumption, designed both to exploit dramatic visual imagery and to foster emotional response.

Post-war the legend grew. The publication of Wing Commander Gibson's *Enemy Coast Ahead*, followed by Paul Brickhill's *The Dam Busters* (itself intended in part to stimulate post-war RAF recruitment) and the subsequent 1955 film served to create a public perception of the operation that was in fact an amalgam of fact, conflation and creative licence.

Left Air Chief Marshal Sir Arthur Harris (left) observes as Wing Commander Guy Gibson's crew is debriefed after No. 617 Squadron's raid on the Ruhr Dams, 16/17 May 1943. *(Air Historical Branch)*

All contributed to a mistaken common belief that the operation was intended severely to cripple industry throughout the Ruhr at a single stroke, thereby decimating armament production and hastening the end of the war. In reality the Dams Raid was seen as being complementary to the then ongoing Battle of the Ruhr, adding to the destruction and dislocation being caused by main force attacks on industrial centres.

While acknowledging that the dams were significant as targets, reports produced by the Ministry of Economic Warfare in April 1943 made a clear distinction between the three main targets and the physical and morale effects that would arise from their destruction. Contrary to popular perception, they were not all 'Ruhr dams'. Only the Möhne and Sorpe Dams lay within the Ruhr. The third and largest target, the Eder, was of minor industrial importance. The primary function of the Möhne was to capture winter rainfall for use during the drier summer period. Destruction might result in overexploitation of ground water supplies, the main source of water for Germany's industrial heartland. Water escaping from the reservoir would inevitably cause considerable damage and disrup-

tion, the amount of which would be dependent upon the level of the reservoir. Back flooding of side valleys before the water reached the main populated areas might moderate the effect, but nevertheless 'the prospects of destruction appear good' and this might be enhanced by constriction in the mid-reaches of the Ruhr Valley, creating a secondary lake that would then drain into lower-lying areas possibly as far as Duisburg. Naturally there would be damage to both industrial and residential property, though the analysts were circumspect, stating that there were too many variables and unknowns to be able to attempt to quantify this, or loss of production.

The additional destruction of the Sorpe Dam would add 50 per cent to the effect of breaching only the Möhne. Between them both dams accounted for 75 per cent of the storage capacity in the Ruhr basin. Conversely, water released by the Eder Dam, whose function was mainly the alleviation of winter flooding and supplementing summer supply for the Mittelland Canal, would initially flood only agricultural land. The only likely industrial effect would be to disrupt production in the low-lying Bettenhausen district of Kassel, 60 miles from the dam. Generation by hydro-electric plants would be reduced and, although useful, this contributed only a small amount and could be offset to a degree by an efficient distribution system.

The reports additionally looked at the potential psychological effect of destruction of the dams. Floods arising from the breaching of the Möhne and Sorpe would affect inhabitants of a densely populated area, who in turn would have large numbers of relatives and friends who would become aware. Those affected by floods from the Eder would

Left The breach in the Möhne Dam four hours after the raid of 16/17 May 1943. *(IWM HU 4594)*

be only a fraction of this number and, since this dam played 'a much less obvious part in the daily lives of large cities', the possibilities for causing alarm and despondency through fear of water shortage would be appreciably less.

This prompts critics of the raid to maintain that the forces available to Chastise were wrongly allocated, and that the primary attacks should have been directed at the Möhne and Sorpe Dams, as prioritized by the planners. However, the Ministry of Economic Warfare analysts were concerned only with the function of the targets and postulating the effect of their destruction. They were not concerned with the practicalities of achieving this. Experiments and Wallis's calculations had focused on the demolition of a gravity dam, and Upkeep had been devised accordingly as a weapon that should achieve a breach of the Möhne Dam after one or two attacks under ideal conditions. It was thus seen as an ideal weapon for the destruction of the Möhne and Eder Dams. Given the likely defences and difficulty in achieving the precise requirements for a perfect release, nine aircraft would be allocated for these two targets in order to give the best chances of success.

The Sorpe was an earthen dam, of greater thickness and with shock-absorbing banks either side of a watertight core. The operation planners acknowledged that it was not the ideal target for Upkeep. However, Wallis believed that the cumulative effect of a number of Upkeeps should be sufficient to damage the dam 'to an extent that would bring about its destruction . . . [which] . . . would be initiated, however, by seepage of water through the watertight wall which formed the central core of the dam and would not be immediately apparent to crews'. Thus, despite the criteria for an accurate attack being thought to be less demanding, Cochrane was still to detail five crews specifically for this one target – in theory sufficient to obtain a breach – although Wallis's additional recommendation that there should be a supplementary attack from 6,000 feet dropping 8,000-pounders on the air side embankment to weaken it (which would have been difficult to orchestrate) was not adopted.

Events would vindicate the numbers allocated to the Möhne and Eder. However, it was a quirk of fate that resulted in the northern wave, detailed to attack the Sorpe, suffering the greatest attrition and resulting in only one attack on this objective, effectively negating its chances of achieving its objective. To allow for such en route attrition the planners had provided an 'airborne reserve' to be directed while over Germany to back up earlier attacks. However, the fog of war intervened and only one out of three aircraft from this reserve wave diverted to the Sorpe was able to make an attack. The two successful attacks were insufficient to cause the level of damage required. Nevertheless it is unjust to suggest that the Sorpe was considered a 'secondary target' and that little consideration was

floods' and, less accurately, 'RAF blow up three dams in Germany'. Speculative descriptions graphically described the likely effects. Post-war examination of the facts found, not surprisingly, that these accounts had created an over inflated impression of major damage. However, the cumulative effects of both this and lesser damage and disruption were without doubt significant. The water had created a continuous path of damage, of varying degrees and effect, through a significant area of the Ruhr. Communications infrastructure was disrupted. Roads and railways, many of which followed the

Right Aerial reconnaissance (vertical) photograph showing the breach in the Möhne Dam caused by No. 617 Squadron, Royal Air Force's raid on 16/17 May 1943. *(Air Historical Branch)*

given to allocating sufficient aircraft for its attack. In defence of the decision not to despatch aircraft to bomb the airside, No. 9 Squadron attacked the Sorpe on 15 October 1944 using 12,000-lb Tallboy deep-penetration bombs (another Wallis brainchild). Despite hits scored on the central core and earth bank, the dam still held.

Wartime press copy made great play of suggesting that large numbers of factories had been swept away or at least inundated, playing up the anticipated damage: 'Floods roar down Ruhr Valley', 'Floods pouring through Ruhr', 'Vast damage by

course of the river, were inundated, bridges washed away, ballast scoured from beneath rail lines. Electricity and telephone cables were swept away, and pumping stations and factory plant rendered inoperable by water and silt, even if the buildings in which they were located remained intact.

Certainly some industrial concerns were soon up and running again, but many at a reduced level of output. In numerous cases water and silt had wrecked machine tools, and replacements had to be sourced from other areas of Germany. Robbing Peter to pay Paul would create a reduction of production elsewhere. Production of armaments requiring specialist steels suffered less than might be expected, but only because even in 1943 Germany had significant steel stocks. However, depletion of these as a result of Chastise imposed further strain on Germany's increasingly beleaguered industrial economy that would impact in the longer term. The attack on the Eder, though of limited industrial effect, accrued perhaps greater results than anticipated by the planners. Large tracts of crops were destroyed and livestock drowned, creating immediate shortages; erosion of fertile topsoil

No effort was spared to speed the repair of the dams – in itself testimony to the importance of the dams to the Germans and justification of their value as targets. However, this rapidity of repair came at a price, creating further difficulties for the Axis war effort. Workers and scarce materials and equipment were withdrawn from projects as far afield as the Atlantic Wall, and other repair work in the Ruhr and other parts of Germany was given secondary importance.

The Ministry of Economic Warfare report had identified that there would be a race against time.

Left A vertical reconnaissance photo showing the breach in the Eder Dam. *(Air Historical Branch)*

would continue to reduce yields for many years to come. There can be no doubt that Chastise made a significant contribution to the Battle of the Ruhr. Post-war, Albert Speer, Hitler's Minister of Armaments, was to write of Chastise: 'That night, employing just a few bombers, the British came close to a success which would have been greater than anything they had achieved hitherto with a commitment of thousands of bombers.'

As the planners had predicted, the Germans reacted swiftly to minimize the effects of Chastise and prevent the disaster from becoming a catastrophe.

Water supplies could be maintained short term by continued underground extraction, but without replenishment from reservoirs, notably the Möhne, overexploitation would cause eventual shortages. Water rationing and the successful reconstruction of the dams by the autumn, permitting the capture of the winter rains, meant that the critical point was never reached. The Möhne was sealed by September 1943 and the Eder in the following month, although work was not fully completed until June 1944. Critics question why no attempt was made to delay the dams' reconstruction – seemingly with

some justification. A few explosive bombs or even incendiaries among the equipment and timber scaffolding might have succeeded in causing significant delay. However, any attacks would have had to be made by main force, bombing from altitude and at night. Unlikely to achieve the precision required to damage the repair sites, an area attack would have been necessary in order to destroy a small target. While bombs that missed might serve to churn up the surrounding area, hindering access, Sir Arthur Harris appears either to have believed such attacks unnecessary, or to have considered that, if large numbers of bombs were going to be dropped in an area attack, then they would be more effective if dropped over an urban target, where each would have a greater chance of inflicting material damage. In any case, the Battle of the Ruhr was soon to conclude, and main force would be seeking other targets.

Assessment of the full impact of Operation Chastise necessitates a much longer view. In revealing the vulnerability of dams to aerial attack, it caused the Germans to instigate defensive measures for other dams throughout Germany. These required not only men, guns and barrage balloons, but also hutting, workers and materials for the construction of other means of defence in the form of steel towers, cables and sea mines (to be detonated to throw up water plumes in the path of any low-flying attacking aircraft). Some 1,500 men were allocated to protect the Möhne and overall over 10,000 men were tasked to defend important dams against attacks that would never materialize.

In one respect it was a pyrrhic victory. Perversely, the success of Chastise created a similar result in Britain. Intelligence reports revealed that, despite the provision of a self-destruct pistol to prevent Upkeep falling into enemy hands, an intact example had been obtained (from the wreckage of Flight Lieutenant Barlow's aircraft). This further increased

Left A (vertical) reconnaissance photo of the Ruhr Valley at Froendenberg-Boesperde, some 13 miles south from the Möhne Dam, showing massive flooding. *(Air Historical Branch)*

concerns already being voiced in certain circles that the Germans might seek to mount a similar attack against British dams, and steps were taken to develop and install protective measures at key reservoirs, including those in the Derwent Valley, used by 617 Squadron in preparation for Chastise. However, no such operation was ever mounted.

Thus in no way can Chastise be dismissed as simply being a propaganda attack. That is not to say that the Ministry of Information and others did not exploit its morale-boosting effects. Not only did it inspire a British audience, the dramatic aerial photographs of the results graphically demonstrated yet again the skill, determination, accuracy and effectiveness of Bomber Command. Ministry of Information Home Intelligence Reports monitored public reaction. News of the operation travelled quickly and was a prime topic of discussion: 'Even in the rural areas of Somerset, where news usually travels slowly, the great event was discussed by farm labourers on their way home from work'. It was seen as a 'brilliant and daring achievement', arousing feelings varying from 'jubilation' to 'grim approval', although 'some later tempered their views with a tinge of horror' at the likely civilian casualties (reported in inflated terms by the press).

Leaflets showing photographs of the breached Möhne Dam were dropped as part of the ongoing campaign to maintain the spirit of those in occupied territories. Winston Churchill was in America at the time of Chastise, seeking to dissuade the Americans from switching their focus from Europe to the Pacific. During a crucial speech to Congress, he referred to the operation as demonstrable proof of the effect that bombing was having on Germany. Likewise it was hoped that Stalin would see it as evidence of the Western Allies' support. Such was the impact of the operation that both Allies requested information on the weapon used and the

nature of the attack. The Ministry of Economic Warfare had hinted at the possibility of 'Black propaganda', and on 20 May a proposal was suggested within the OSS Morale Operations Branch to start a rumour in the Ruhr that the water supply for two years had been lost and that drinking water supply had become hopelessly contaminated, resulting in an epidemic of typhoid and intestinal diseases.

Strengthened defences would make further attacks against German dams impracticable. This did not prevent the planners looking elsewhere and seeking new and different targets for Upkeep. Attacks on Italian dams were considered as a means of assisting the Allied invasion of southern Europe, weirs and locks were examined as a way of disrupting inland waterway communications, as were embanked stretches of canals. However, there were only limited aircraft modified to carry the store and few crews trained in its use. The possibility of heavy losses in any future operation prompted caution. Likely targets were either discounted, for practical, tactical or political reasons, or, as in the case of the Rothensee ship lift and strategic railway viaducts, held back in anticipation of Tallboy and Grand

Slam. Paradoxically, then, the success of Upkeep, in creating the support for the progression of Wallis's deep-penetration bomb, came to hobble its own future use.

Today the operation would be considered disproportionate and counter-productive in modern warfare, where post-conflict reconstruction figures significantly in the planning and evaluation process. It would also contravene the International Law of Armed Conflict: the 1949 Geneva Convention provides protection from the attack on dams, dykes, nuclear power stations and other works or installations containing dangerous forces, which would cause flooding resulting in civilian losses. While the operation was never specifically intended to drown civilians, it would have been naive to overlook the fact that success would inevitably result in significant loss of human life. Eleven nights earlier, a force of 596 aircraft had attacked Dortmund, causing 693 fatalities, the heaviest to date. The total attributed to Chastise, conducted by 19 aircraft of which only 10 made attacks, was 1,294 deaths. With a few local exceptions, such as that at Himmelpforten, a few miles down the valley from the Möhne Dam, there were no specific alarms to warn of an attack on the dam, or impending flood. Air-raid warnings in the vicinity of the dams naturally induced people to take shelter, often in cellars. Many, including 493 foreign workers in a labour camp on the outskirts of Neheim, below the Möhne, must have drowned oblivious of the danger until the final moments.

And what of the aircrew survivors of Operation Chastise? One hundred and thirty-three aircrew took part in the raid. Fifty-three died and three were taken prisoner of war. Of the seventy-seven survivors returning to Scampton on the morning of 17 May, only forty-five would survive the war.

With his rear turret out of action, compass difficulties and time running out, Flight Sergeant Cyril Anderson had made the decision to return with his Upkeep to Scampton. It was a decision that Gibson, exhausted after six and a half hours in the air, during which he had seen his friend John Hopgood die, found difficult to accept. After a short, sharp interview, Anderson and his crew were posted from the squadron and returned to operations with No. 49 Squadron at Fiskerton. Arriving back from an operation to Mannheim on the night of 23/24 September 1943, their aircraft was brought down by a nightfighter. There were no survivors.

David Maltby and his crew were killed on 14/15 September 1943. Flying at low level over the North Sea for an operation against the Dortmund-Ems Canal (an operation originally conceived further to employ Upkeep), his aircraft was seen to hit the water and explode as the aircraft turned for home after the force was recalled on account of bad weather. The following night the squadron was despatched against the same target. It was to prove disastrous. Five out of eight aircraft failed to return, including Flying Officer William Divall and Flight Lieutenant Harold Wilson, who had trained for, but not participated in, Chastise. Les Knight made the supreme sacrifice after his aircraft hit trees at low level in the target area. Staying at the controls of his badly damaged aircraft to allow his crew to escape (all survived, five making successful evasions and 'home runs' to the UK), he died when his Lancaster struck an obstruction and exploded as he tried to execute a belly landing near Den Ham, Holland. Dennis Powell, along with, Robert

Hutchison, 'Terry' Taerum and George Deering from Wing Commander Gibson's Chastise crew would also die that night, flying with Squadron Leader George Holden, the new squadron commander, brought down by flak over the town of Nordhorn.

Immediately following the Dortmund-Ems Canal operation, Mick Martin was given temporary command of the squadron for two months, until Leonard Cheshire arrived. Martin helped Cheshire develop an accurate low-level marking technique, but his aircraft was damaged, and his bomb aimer Flight Lieutenant Bob Hay killed, during an attack on the Antheor Viaduct, near Cannes, on 12/13 February 1944. On his return Martin agreed to be posted – only soon to engineer a return to operational flying as a highly successful Mosquito intruder pilot with No. 515 Squadron. He finally retired in 1974, having attained the rank of Air Marshal, and died in 1988. His penultimate posting as Commander-in-Chief RAF Germany saw him in effect responsible for the defence of the Möhne Dam. John Pulford, Wing Commander Gibson's flight engineer, died the same day as Hay.

Left The Möhne Dam – 2013. (*Fighting High*)

Right The cross at the lip of the crater marking the crash site of P/O Ottley's Lancaster – a few miles north of Kötterberg, north of Hamm, Germany. (Inset) Plaque at the crash site of P/O Ottley's Lancaster. *(Fighting High)*

IN MEMORY OF THE CREW
LANCASTER ED910 AJ-C

P/O	W.OTTLEY DFC	PILOT
SGT.	R.MARSDEN	F/ENG.
F/O	J.BARRETT DFC	NAV.
SGT.	J.GUTERMAN DFM	W/OP
F/SGT.	T.B.JOHNSTON	B/A
SGT.	F.TEES (SURVIVOR)	R/G
SGT.	H.STRANGE	F/G

617 SQUADRON RAF
DAMS RAID 17th MAY 1943

He was flying with Squadron Leader Bill Suggitt, and his aircraft had returned to an advanced operating base at Ford. After refuelling, the crew took off in poor visibility to return to Woodhall Spa, but some ten minutes after take-off the aircraft struck a cloud-shrouded hilltop at Upwaltham, Sussex, killing all on board.

Bill Townsend and his crew (with the exception of his wireless operator, George Chalmers, and Flight Engineer Edward Smith) were posted from the squadron as tour expired in September 1943. After a period instructing, Townsend would be posted to a Liberator Conversion Unit in India.

Chalmers continued with the squadron for another twenty-three operations until he was posted in July 1944. Townsend's two gunners, Doug Webb and Ray Wilkinson, would return to the squadron in October 1944, remaining with it until the end of the war.

On 20/21 December 1943 Geoff Rice, who had survived hitting the water over the Zuider Zee on his way to the Sorpe Dam, was shot from the sky while returning from an abortive raid on Liege. His aircraft disintegrated in mid-air, and Rice was the only survivor from the crew, suffering with a broken wrist. After evading capture for several months with the Belgian Resistance, Rice was finally betrayed and taken prisoner of war.

Brian Jagger, Shannon's front gunner, was posted to the Bombing Development Unit at Feltwell at the beginning of March 1944, only to be killed some seven weeks later in a flying accident during a fighter affiliation exercise. Ken Brown was posted from the squadron to No. 5 Lancaster Finishing School as an instructor in March 1944, having completed eleven more operations with the squadron. He died in December 2002. Wing Commander Gibson's rear gunner, Richard Trevor Roper, was posted from the squadron in August 1943, but returned to operations with No. 97 Squadron at the beginning of March 1944. Within a month he was dead, his aircraft falling victim to nightfighter attack, one of the ninety-five aircraft lost in the notorious raid against Nuremberg on 30/31 March 1944.

David Shannon, Joe McCarthy and Les Munro continued to operate with the squadron, each being promoted to squadron leader, until June 1944, when the trio were posted as tour expired – the last of the captains who had flown on Chastise. All survived the war. Leaving the service but remaining in the UK post-war, David Shannon spent a period farming before becoming a successful executive in the oil industry. Tragically he would die in 1993, one month before the 50th Anniversary of Chastise. Joe McCarthy ended the war at the Royal Aircraft Establishment, Farnborough, test flying captured German aircraft. He remained in the RCAF until the late 1960s, in retirement dealing in real estate and lecturing at the USAF War College, Maxwell AFB. He died in September 1998.

Wing Commander Gibson was detached from the squadron in August 1943 to take part in a public-relations tour of North America. On his return he was attached to the RAF Accident Investigation Branch, during which time he wrote a large section of *Enemy Coast Ahead*, before being sent on a Staff Course at Bulstrode Park. He was then posted as a member of the Base Staff at No. 55 Base, East Kirkby, before being transferred as Base Operations Officer at No. 54 Base, Conningsby, Base Station for Woodhall Spa, from which No. 617 Squadron was now flying. Frustrated by being surrounded by operational crews yet officially forbidden to operate himself, he seized an opportunity that placed him in the position of nominating himself as master bomber for a raid against the dual centres of München Gladbach/Rheydt on 19 September 1944. After he had directed a difficult attack, his Mosquito headed for home, but crashed at Steenbergen in Holland, killing Gibson and his navigator, Squadron Leader James Warwick.

Today, seventy years on, only three veterans of Chastise remain: Les Munro, back in his native New Zealand, Canadian Fred Sutherland, who made a successful evasion after his escape from Les Knight's damaged aircraft over Holland, and, in the UK, George 'Johnny' Johnson. Now all in their 90s, they still maintain strong links with the squadron they helped to form, their diverse locations and nationalities striking an appropriate note to commemorate the squadron's initial membership of 90 RAF, 29 RCAF, 2 RNZAF and 12 RAAF aircrew members: the original 'Dam Busters'. ●

Left At the end of the Second World War the remains of thousands of Bomber Command airmen, who had been killed on operations, were brought to the Reichswald Forest War Cemetery from cemeteries and other burial locations. Included were the bodies of those killed from four of the crews lost on the Dam Busters raid. (*Fighting High*)

OPERATION CHASTISE
ROLL OF HONOUR

**ARTHUR, Warrant Officer II
(Bomb Aimer) James
Lamb, R119416 RCAF**

17 May 1943. Age 25

Bergen-op-Zoom War Cemetery,
Netherlands, Collective Grave,
Plot 24, Row B, Graves 5–7
Lancaster ED865 AJ-S (Pilot Officer
Burpee)

**ASTELL, Flight Lieutenant
(Pilot) William, 60283 DFC,
RAFVR**

17 May 1943. Age 23

Reichswald Forest War Cemetery,
Germany, Plot 21, Row D, Grave 13
Think not of me as dead.
Happy he whose course is sped.
He has gone home to God.
Lancaster ED864 AJ-B

**BARLOW, Flight Lieutenant
(Pilot) Robert Norman
George, A401899 DFC, RAAF**

16 May 1943. Age 32

Reichswald Forest War Cemetery,
Germany, Plot 5, Row C, Grave 9
In loving memory of my husband who gave
all for his country.
Lancaster ED927 AJ-E

**BARRETT, Flying Officer
(Navigator) Jack Kenneth,
115775 DFC, RAFVR**

17 May 1943. Age 22

Reichswald Forest War Cemetery,
Germany, Plot 31, Row F, Grave 14
Grant him, O Lord, safe lodging,
Holy rest and peace at the last.
Lancaster ED910 AJ-C
(Pilot Officer Ottley)

**BOLITHO, Sergeant
(Air Gunner) Richard
1211045 RAFVR**

17 May 1943. Age 23

Reichswald Forest War Cemetery,
Germany, Plot 21, Row E, Grave 1
Greater love hath no man than this, that
a man lay down his life for his friends.
Lancaster ED864 AJ-B (Flight
Lieutenant Astell)

**BRADY, Warrant Officer II
(Air Gunner) Joseph Gordon,
R93554 RCAF**

17 May 1943. Age 27

Bergen-op-Zoom War Cemetery
Netherlands, Plot 23, Row A, Grave 1
Lancaster ED865 AJ-S (Pilot Officer
Burpee)

**BRENNAN, Sergeant
(Flight Engineer) Charles,
942037 RAFVR**

17 May 1943

Rheinberg War Cemetery, Germany,
Collective Grave, Plot 17, Row E,
Graves 2–6
Lancaster ED925 AJ-M
(Flight Lieutenant Hopgood)

BURGESS, Flying Officer (Navigator) Philip Sidney, 124881 RAFVR

16 May 1943. Age 20

Reichswald Forest War Cemetery, Germany, Plot 5, Row C, Grave 7
Greater love hath no man than this that a man lay down his life for his friends.
Lancaster ED927 AJ-E
(Flight Lieutenant Barlow)

BURPEE, Pilot Officer (Pilot) Lewis Johnstone, J17115 DFM, RCAF

17 May 1943. Age 25

Bergen-op-Zoom War Cemetery, Netherlands, Plot 23, Row B, Grave 3
Into the mosaic of victory we placed our most precious piece. Wife and son.
Lancaster ED865 AJ-S

BURROWS, Sergeant (Air Gunner) Norman Rupert, 1503094 RAFVR

17 May 1943

Reichswald Forest War Cemetery, Germany, Plot 5, Row C, Grave 2.
Lancaster ED937 AJ-Z
(Squadron Leader Maudslay)

BYERS, Pilot Officer (Pilot) Vernon William, J17474 RCAF

16 May 1943. Age 23

Runnymede Memorial, Panel 175
Lancaster ED934 AJ-K

COTTAM, Warrant Officer II (Wireless Operator/AG) Alden Preston, R93558 RCAF

17 May 1943. Age 30

Reichswald Forest War Cemetery, Germany. Plot 5, Row C, Grave 1
He gave his life that we might live. Ever in our thoughts, Mum, Dad and Sisters.
Lancaster ED937 AJ-Z
(Squadron Leader Maudslay)

EARNSHAW, Flying Officer (Navigator) Kenneth, J10891 RCAF

17 May 1943

Rheinberg War Cemetery, Germany, Collective Grave, Plot 17, Row E, Graves 2–6
Lancaster ED925 AJ-M
(Flight Lieutenant Hopgood)

FULLER, Pilot Officer (Navigator/ Bomb Aimer) Michael John David, 143760 RAFVR

17 May 1943. Age 23

Reichswald Forest War Cemetery, Germany, Collective Grave, Plot 5, Row B, Graves 16–18
We have gained a peace, unshaken by pain forever.
Lancaster ED937 AJ-Z
(Squadron Leader Maudslay)

GARBAS, Flight Sergeant (Air Gunner) Francis Anthony R103201 RCAF

17 May 1943

Reichswald Forest War Cemetery, Germany, Collective Grave, Plot 21, Row D, Graves 16–18
Lancaster ED864 AJ-B
(Flight Lieutenant Astell)

GARSHOWITZ, Warrant Officer II (Wireless Operator/AG) Abram, R84377 RCAF

17 May 1943

Reichswald Forest War Cemetery, Germany, Collective Grave, Plot 21, Row D, Graves 16–18
Lancaster ED864 AJ-B
(Flight Lieutenant Astell)

GILLESPIE, Pilot Officer (Bomb Aimer) Alan, 144205 DFM, RAFVR

16 May 1943. Age 20

Reichswald Forest War Cemetery, Germany, Plot 5, Row C, Grave 10
At the going down of the sun and in the morning we will remember them.
Lancaster ED927 AJ-E
(Flight Lieutenant Barlow)

GLINZ, Flying Officer (Air Gunner) Harvey Sterling, J10212 RCAF

16 May 1943. Age 22

Reichswald Forest War Cemetery, Germany, Plot 5, Row C, Grave 8
Always Remembered.
Lancaster ED927 AJ-E
(Flight Lieutenant Barlow)

GREGORY, Flying Officer (Air Gunner) George Henry Ford Goodwin, 141285 DFM, RAFVR

17 May 1943

Rheinberg War Cemetery, Germany, Collective Grave, Plot 17, Row E, Graves 2–6
Lancaster ED925 AJ-M
(Flight Lieutenant Hopgood)

GUTERMAN, Sergeant (Wireless Operator/AG) Jack, 1172550 DFM, RAFVR

17 May 1943. Age 23

Reichswald Forest War Cemetery, Germany, Plot 31, Row F, Grave 12
A devoted son and a loving brother.
Lancaster ED910 AJ-C.
(Pilot Officer Ottley)

HOPGOOD, Flight Lieutenant (Pilot) John Vere, 61281 DFC and Bar, RAFVR

17 May 1943. Age 21

Rheinberg War Cemetery, Germany, Collective Grave, Plot 17, Row E, Graves 2–6
Lancaster ED925 AJ-M

HOPKINSON, Flying Officer (Bomb Aimer) Donald, 127817 RAFVR

17 May 1943. Age 22

Reichswald Forest War Cemetery, Germany, Collective Grave, Plot 21, Row D, Graves 16–18
He died to give us another dawn.
For us to live all his tomorrows.
Lancaster ED864 AJ-B
(Flight Lieutenant Astell)

HORSFALL, Sergeant (Flight Engineer) David Taylor, 568924 RAF

17 May 1943. Age 23

Bergen General Cemetery, Netherlands, Plot 2, Row D, Grave 5
Lancaster ED887 AJ-A
(Squadron Leader Young)

IBBOTSON, Sergeant (Air Gunner) Wilfred, 655431 RAFVR

17 May 1943. Age 29

Bergen General Cemetery, Netherlands, Plot 2, Row D, Grave 6
Heavenly stars shine on the grave of one we loved but could not save.
Lancaster ED887 AJ-A
(Squadron Leader Young)

JARVIE, Sergeant (Air Gunner) Charles McAllister, 1058757 RAFVR

16 May 1943. Age 21

Runnymede Memorial, Panel 154
Lancaster ED934 AJ-K
(Pilot Officer Byers)

JAYE, Sergeant (Navigator) Thomas, 1299446 RAFVR

17 May 1943

Bergen-op-Zoom War Cemetery, Netherlands, Collective Grave, Plot 24, Row B, Graves 5–7
We loved him and we miss him yet, our hearts still sore, we can't forget.
Lancaster ED865 AJ-S
(Pilot Officer Burpee)

JOHNSTON, Flight Sergeant

(Bomb Aimer) Thomas Barr,

1060657 RAFVR

17 May 1943

Reichswald Forest War Cemetery,
Germany, Plot 31, Row F, Grave 15
In ever loving memory of my dear son
Thomas Barr. God's will be done.
Lancaster ED910 AJ-C
(Pilot Officer Ottley)

KINNEAR, Sergeant

(Flight Engineer) John,

635123 RAF

17 May 1943. Age 21

Reichswald Forest War Cemetery,
Germany, Plot 21, Row D, Grave 14
My race is run, my warfare's o'er.
Lancaster ED864 AJ-B
(Flight Lieutenant Astell)

LIDDELL, Sergeant

(Air Gunner) Jack Robert

George,

1338282 RAFVR

16 May 1943. Age 18

Reichswald Forest War Cemetery,
Germany, Plot 5, Row C, Grave 5
In the prime of his youth,
he died that we might live.
Lancaster ED927 AJ-E
(Flight Lieutenant Barlow)

LONG, Sergeant

(Air Gunner) William Charles

Arthur,

1600540 RAFVR

17 May 1943. Age 19

Bergen-op-Zoom War Cemetery,
Netherlands, Collective Grave,
Plot 24, Row B, Graves 5–7
In undying memory of our dearly loved
son Bill. 'Greater love hath no man.'
Lancaster ED865 AJ-S
(Pilot Officer Burpee)

MacCAUSLAND, Flying Officer

(Air Observer) Vincent Sanford,

J15309 RCAF

17 May 1943. Age 30

Bergen General Cemetery,
Netherlands, Plot 2, Row D, Grave 3
In loving memory. Faithful in duty:
Courageous in battle: Brave in death.
At rest.
Lancaster ED887 AJ-A
(Squadron Leader Young)

McDOWELL, Flight Sergeant

(Air Gunner) James,

R101749 RCAF

16 May 1943

Harlingen General Cemetery,
Netherlands, Plot E, Row 4,
Grave 11
Lancaster ED934 AJ-K
(Pilot Officer Byers)

MARRIOTT, Sergeant
(Flight Engineer) John,
1003474 DFM, RAFVR

17 May 1943. Age 23

Reichswald Forest War Cemetery,
Germany, Plot 5, Row C, Grave 4
Lancaster ED937 AJ-Z
(Squadron Leader Maudslay)

MARSDEN, Sergeant
(Flight Engineer) Ronald,
568415 RAF

17 May 1943. Age 23

Reichswald Forest War Cemetery,
Germany, Plot 31, Row F, Grave 10
*To be with him in the same old way is our
dearest wish today. Dad, Mam and family.*
Lancaster ED910 AJ-C
(Pilot Officer Ottley)

MAUDSLAY, Squadron Leader
(Pilot) Henry Eric,
62275 DFC, RAFVR

17 May 1943. Age 21

Reichswald Forest War Cemetery,
Germany, Plot 5, Row C, Grave 3
*He died gloriously in the breaching of the
Eder Dam.*
Lancaster ED937 AJ-Z

MINCHIN, Sergeant
(Wireless Operator/AG) John
William
1181097 RAFVR

17 May 1943. Age 27

Rheinberg War Cemetery, Germany,
Collective Grave, Plot 17, Row E,
Graves 2–6
Lancaster ED925 AJ-M
(Flight Lieutenant Hopgood)

NICHOLS, Sergeant
(Wireless Operator/AG)
Lawrence William,
1377941 RAFVR

17 May 1943. Age 33

Bergen General Cemetery,
Netherlands, Plot 2, Row E, Grave 28
*Loved by all sadly missed. Remembering
also the gallant crew who went with him.*
Lancaster ED887 AJ-A
(Squadron Leader Young)

OTTLEY, Pilot Officer
(Pilot) Warner,
141460 DFC, RAFVR

17 May 1943

Reichswald Forest War Cemetery,
Germany, Plot 31, Row F, Grave 11
Lancaster ED910 AJ-C

PEGLER, Sergeant
(Flight Engineer) Guy,
573474 RAF

17 May 1943. Age 21

Bergen-op-Zoom War Cemetery,
Netherlands, Collective Grave,
Plot 24, Row B, Graves 5–7
Lancaster ED865 AJ-S
(Pilot Officer Burpee)

ROBERTS, Flight Sergeant
(Navigator) Charles Walpole,
1269945 RAFVR

17 May 1943

Bergen General Cemetery,
Netherlands, Plot 2, Row E, Grave 17
Lancaster ED887 AJ-A
(Squadron Leader Young)

STRANGE, Sergeant

(Air Gunner) Harry John,

1395453 RAFVR

17 May 1943. Age 20

Reichswald Forest War Cemetery,
Germany, Plot 31, Row F, Grave 13
A silent thought, a private tear.
In my memory ever dear.
Lancaster ED910 AJ-C
(Pilot Officer Ottley)

TAYLOR, Sergeant

(Flight Engineer) Alastair

James,

575430 RAF

16 May 1943. Age 20

Runnymede Memorial, Panel 166.
Lancaster ED934 AJ-K.
(Pilot Officer Byers)

TYTHERLEIGH, Flying Officer

(Air Gunner) William John,

120851 DFC, RAFVR

17 May 1943. Age 21

Reichswald Forest War Cemetery,
Germany, Communal Grave,
Plot 5, Row B, Graves 16–18
Good night, son, God bless.
We shall see you in the morning.
Lancaster ED937 AJ-Z
(Squadron Leader Maudslay)

URQUHART, Pilot Officer

(Navigator) Robert Alexander,

J9763 DFC, RCAF

17 May 1943. Age 23

Reichswald Forest War Cemetery,
Germany, Communal Grave, Plot 5,
Row B, Graves 16–18
Lancaster ED937 AJ-Z
(Squadron Leader Maudslay)

WARNER, Flying Officer

(Navigator) James Herbert

128619 RAFVR

16 May 1943

Runnymede Memorial, Panel 130
Lancaster ED934 AJ-K
(Pilot Officer Byers)

WELLER, Pilot Officer

(Wireless Operator/AG)

Leonard George,

142507 RAFVR

17 May 1943. Age 28

Bergen-op-Zoom War Cemetery,
Netherlands, Plot 27, Row A, Grave 6
In loving memory of a devoted husband
and father.
Lancaster ED865 AJ-S
(Pilot Officer Burpee)

WHILLIS, Pilot Officer (Flight Engineer) Samuel Leslie, 144619 RAFVR

16 May 1943. Age 31

Reichswald Forest War Cemetery, Germany, Plot 5, Row C, Grave 6
Greater love hath no man than this, that a man lay down his life for his friends.
Lancaster ED927 AJ-E
(Flight Lieutenant Barlow)

WHITAKER, Pilot Officer (Bomb Aimer) Arthur Neville 144777 RAF

16 May 1943

Runnymede Memorial, Panel 134
Lancaster ED934 AJ-K
(Pilot Officer Byers)

WILE, Pilot Officer (Navigator) Floyd Alvin, J16872 RCAF

17 May 1943. Age 24

Reichswald Forest War Cemetery, Germany, Plot 21, Row D, Grave 15
Gone but not forgotten.
Lancaster ED864 AJ-B
(Flight Lieutenant Astell)

WILKINSON, Sergeant (Wireless Operator/AG) John, 1025280 RAFVR

16 May 1943. Age 21

Runnymede Memorial, Panel 169
Lancaster ED934 AJ-K
(Pilot Officer Byers)

WILLIAMS, Flying Officer (Wireless Operator/AG) Charles Rowland, 405224 DFC, RAAF

16 May 1943. Age 34

Reichswald Forest War Cemetery, Germany, Plot 5, Row C, Grave 11
He gallantly died renouncing all the things that he loved.
Lancaster ED927 AJ-E
(Flight Lieutenant Barlow)

YEO, Sergeant (Air Gunner) Gordon Arthur, 1317656 RAFVR

17 May 1943. Age 20

Bergen General Cemetery, Netherlands, Plot 2, Row D, Grave 2
At the going down of the sun and in the morning we will remember him.
Lancaster ED887 AJ-A
(Squadron Leader Young)

YOUNG, Squadron Leader (Pilot) Henry Melvin, 72478 DFC and Bar, RAFVR

17 May 1943. Age 27

Bergen General Cemetery, Netherlands, Plot 2, Row D, Grave 4
Lancaster ED887 AJ-A

PRISONER OF WAR

BURCHER, Pilot Officer (Air Gunner) Anthony Fisher A403182 DFM, RAAF

FTR 17 May 1943

PoW No. 1341, Stalag Luft III, Sagan
Lancaster ED925 AJ-M
(Flight Lieutenant Hopgood)

FRASER, Flight Sergeant (Air Bomber) John William, J17696 RCAF

FTR 17 May 1943

PoW No. 136, Stalag Luft VI, later Stalag Luft III, Sagan
Lancaster ED925 AJ-M
(Flight Lieutenant Hopgood)

TEES, Sergeant (Air Gunner) Frank, 1333270 RAFVR

FTR 17 May 1943

PoW No. 42790, 9C, Stalag Luft VI, Heydekrug and Stalag Luft III, Sagan
Lancaster ED910 AJ-C
(Pilot Officer Ottley)

ACKNOWLEDGEMENTS
AND NOTES

The publisher would like to thank Sebastian Cox and Lee Barton of the Air Historical Branch for their assistance with photographs.

Introduction, Chapters Two and Four, Postscript, Roll of Honour (Robert Owen)
These accounts draw upon material gathered over many years and I would like to acknowledge all who have contributed to my research. In particular I would like to express my appreciation to Ray Hepner for his generosity in making available his collection of documents and photographs relating to Bill Astell, and to Simon Muggleton and Steve Darlow for material relevant to Robert Urquhart. Over many years Richard Morris and Dr John Sweetman have stimulated debate and provided new insights.
My grateful thanks go also to Sebastian Cox and the staff of Air Historical Branch and additionally to Peter Elliott and his team in the Department of Research and Information Services at the RAF Museum for their continued support and professional advice.

Finally, and in no small measure, my gratitude is extended to past and present members of No. 617 Squadron and its Association for over 45 years' help, encouragement and continued fellowship.

Chapter One (Steve Darlow)
With thanks to the National Archives of Canada for access to their archives, and to Ken Joyce who carried out the Canadian research. I also extend my appreciation to Bomber Command navigator Gordon Mellor, for giving up his time to discuss the intricacies of night time navigation in a wartime setting.

Research for this book reveals an inconsistency with regard Vernon Byers' age. His personal papers, at the National Archives of Canada, consistently show a date of birth as 24 September 1919, corresponding with details of his schooling. However, the Commonwealth War Graves Commission website shows Vernon's age at death as 32. We believe this is in error and Vernon was 23 when he lost his life on the Dams Raid.

Chapter Three (Sean Feast)
I would like to record the sterling support of Shere Fraser McCarthy in bringing together the story of her father, John Fraser, and Tony Burcher. Her help in providing letters and photographs from that time were invaluable in being able to piece together their story. I would also like to highlight that John Fraser's logbook remains 'missing', as do the logbooks of Ken Earnshaw and Gordon Yeo. If the reader has any knowledge of their whereabouts, as we celebrate the 70th anniversary of the Dam Busters raid, perhaps now would be the perfect time to ensure their rightful return to their respective families.

Chapter Five (Arthur Thorning)
I must start by thanking Mrs Clare Hopkins, Archivist, Trinity College, Oxford, who asked me to write a biographical note on Melvin Young for the 2003 College Report, thus starting my research and interest in his story, culminating in a full biography published by Pen and Sword in 2008, *The Dam Buster who Cracked the Dam – the Story of Melvin 'Dinghy' Young*. I must also thank Clare for her continuing support and for finding much source material, which now resides in the College archives. The majority of the illustrations for this chapter are reproduced by permission of the President and Fellows of Trinity College, Oxford.

I also wish to thank most sincerely Melvin's family who were both encouraging and supportive. In particular: his late sister Mrs Angela Sturr (Dr Angela Rowan Young, MD); his brother-in-law Mr Edward Rawson; his niece by marriage, the late Rebecca Rawson, who generously provided invaluable material left by Melvin's wife Priscilla; and the late Mr Dodd Young, his adopted brother.

INDEX

124